STOP
OVERTHINKING

DISCOVER HYPNOSIS TO FIGHT ANXIETY,
STOP PANIC ATTACKS, START TO SLEEP
BETTER AND LIVE HAPPY. BOOST
POSITIVE THINKING, GET FREE FROM
NEGATIVE THOUGHTS AND INCREASE
YOUR SELF-ESTEEM

ERIKA YOUNG

TABLE OF CONTENTS

INTRODUCTION..6

1.   OVERTHINKING 12

2.   SYMPTOMS OF AN OVERTHINKER 18

3.   WHAT ARE STRESS AND ANXIETY?................................24

4.   DECLUTTER YOUR MIND TO CLEAN YOUR THOUGHTS 34

5.   TECHNIQUES OF GUIDED MEDITATION TO QUIT ANXIETY 46

6.   MEDITATIVE BREATHING TECHNIQUES 56

7.   WHAT IS HYPNOSIS ? 62

8.   SELF-HYPNOSIS SESSIONS 72

9.   DEEP SLEEP HYPNOSIS SESSIONS 82

10.   HYPNOSIS FOR OVERTHINKING.................................. 92

11.   HYPNOSIS FOR PROCRASTINATION 98

12.   HOW TO CALM EMOTIONS... 104

13.   THOUGHTS ABOUT CALMING YOUR WORRIES AND ANXIETY . 116

14.   LACK OF SELF ESTEEM 122

15.   LACK OF SELF-ESTEEM CAN CAUSE OVERTHINKING 128

16.   THE IMPORTANCE OF SELF-LOVE FOR YOUR LIFE 140

17.   "IF YOU WANT IT, YOU'LL TAKE IT": THE IMPORTANCE OF POSITIVE THINKING AND SETTING GOALS 148

18.   EXCERCISE TO GAIN SELF-ESTEEM 156

19.   IMPROVE RELATIONSHIPS BETWEEN MYSELF AND OTHERS: THE RIGHT WAY TO LOOK AT OTHERS...................................... 162

20.   THE OPINION THAT MATTERS IS YOUR OWN: LEARN TO THINK ALL BY YOURSELF.. 172

21.   OVERCOMING NEGATIVE THINKING 176

22.   LAW OF ATTRACTION TO IMPROVE YOUR LIFE 186

23. QUICK AND PRACTICAL SELF-ESTEEM BOOSTING TIPS............**192**

24. HOW SELF-HYPNOSIS CAN INCREASE OUR SELF-ESTEEM AND CONFIDENCE **196**

25. SELF HYPNOSIS SESSION **204**

26. DEEP SLEEP HYPNOSIS SESSION...................................... **208**

CONCLUSION...**214**

Stop Overthinking

Introduction

Have you ever felt restless and couldn't sleep even after a very tiring and loaded day? You keep on thinking about your problems on work or in your relationships? Even tried taking on sleeping pills and other drugs that may help you fall asleep? Well, you are not alone in feeling that way. In fact, many people experience anxiety and stress that leads to insomnia. With this, we can help you and guide you throughout the process in order to help you out with this problem.

Anxiety or depression can make a person feel paralyzed over seemingly manageable situations. Do you ever think why you worry over things? Well, the reality is that the worry emanates from your mind other than the predicament or situation you are facing. The mind and body connection leads to physical impacts when one has an anxiety attack. Worrying causes fatigue, insomnia, muscle tension, irritability, twitching, digestive problems, and startled responses. While you might argue that the symptoms you experience are manageable, it is crucial to seek medical intervention and other non-intrusive relaxation approaches that will enable you to lead a healthy life. When you anticipate the worst in all situations, you might be unable to have healthy relationships, and your productivity dwindles. The condition makes people withdraw and treat their acquaintances with the utmost suspicion.

Anxiety can be an intense and overwhelming feeling. Be assured that you are not battling the condition alone. Millions of people worldwide suffer from an anxiety disorder. Notably, there is a difference between feeling anxious and clinical anxiety. The former can manifest through signs such as sweaty palms, chest tightness, stomach upsets, headaches, or heart palpitations. The occurrences result from the pumping of adrenaline. Anxiety as a disorder makes one experience excessive and persistent worry. In such instances, a person has no rational perspective and usually have unwarranted concerns. To manage anxiety, you will need a deep understanding of the condition.

Illustratively, an anxious mind equates to a room with thousands of drunken and unruly monkeys. The monkeys chatter endlessly and jump around without a care in the world. The highest voice of the clamoring monkeys is that of fear. This monkey is ever creating alarms in any slight situation. It creates thousands of 'what-if' scenarios, making anxious thoughts stay at our minds' forefronts. Fighting the monkeys can be tasking because they are an integral part of our consciousness. While we cannot banish these monkeys because they are part of us, we can tame them. Meditation allows you to listen and understand the chattering monkeys. Each meditation session familiarizes you with the good and bad behaviors of the monkey. You also get to understand their trigger points. Once you are the master, they learn to submit, and you can build a trusting and mutual relationship. Ultimately, you will enjoy calmness and happiness.

Meditation stops the perpetual chatter within our skulls. Thinking all the time can make one live in illusions. Meditation quiets an overactive mind. Learn to identify with the silence between all your mental actions. Meditation should be a regular practice that will help you realize that you are not your feelings or thoughts. The effectiveness of this practice is gradual, which makes it more sustainable than most medications. The detachment resulting from meditation allows you to rest in your being. Through meditation, you can address external triggers that threaten to disorient your inner peace. With intentionality, you can learn the meditation skills and use them at your convenient time or place. Whether you are on tranquilizers or any other medication that calms your nerves, meditation can be a complimentary practice you don't want to ignore.

Self-hypnosis is a mental tool which you can use to carve your own personality and destiny. You can become anything you like. You can choose to become like your role model or you can choose to be an improved version of yourself. You can attract anything in your life you want to have through the process of self-hypnosis. No doubt, action is the foundation of all success and hard-work is the basis of all achievement. However, the constant motivation required to be proactive all the time can be provided by the self-hypnosis. It also provides you the persistence and perseverance required in making hard-work effective. The "inspired action" and "goal oriented motivation" are the key outcomes of self-hypnosis. Finally, since it is already established that there are endless possibilities for a human being, you only have to decide what you want to make possible for you and it will surely be possible. The best thing that you should make possible in your life is the one that makes you happy because if you follow your bliss, then everything in this universe conspires to make that path to your destination easier to follow and your goal easier to achieve. I wish you a happy journey of life ahead.

Who says that you must be a perfectionist to be successful in life? It will only make it more difficult for you to reach your goals. For example, a perfectionistic person trying to lose weight might become so careful about what he/she eats, how he/she trains, etc. that he/she might lose sight of his/her real goals.

You don't need to be perfect to reach your goals; you only need to keep putting in the necessary effort to achieve success. What does this involve? Cultivate virtues like patience. Trust your abilities and be consistent. If you take the perfectionistic route, you will always find something you're not doing right each day; you will be focusing negatively on what you don't want. This will not help you to achieve positive outcomes.

Instead of striving for perfection, address each day as they come, work hard, and focus positively on achieving your goals. In the long run, you will achieve what you set out to do, but, in the meantime, keep finding ways to improve, to be just a little bit today than you were yesterday.

The truth is, people can be so critical. Despite your efforts, some people will never appreciate anything you do or achieve. Negative, critical feedback may make you feel scared or less confident; you may feel as if you are not anywhere close to success. Overcoming such feelings can be extremely difficult.

It is impossible to know exactly what others are thinking. Remember, everyone may see a different version of you, depending on what they choose to look at and the cognitive biases that they possess. Often, how they perceive you may not have anything to do with who you really are. Also, their opinions may change, depending on a multitude of different factors.

So, difficult as it often is, you need to try to worry less about what others think about you. If people find what you are doing interesting, that's great! If they don't, it is not a reflection on you and how interesting you really are. You need to be able develop an opinion of yourself that is independent of what others think of you, and this is something that many people struggle with.

Many won't care about what we do; everyone has a right to determine their own priorities, goals, wants, and needs. You deserve to have a life that is appealing by your own standards, not just society's.

The world of the self is full of different characteristics and textures. You must have heard the phrase 'self-esteem' being mentioned by prominent psychologists and experts quite a lot. Such is the importance of this phrase that from workplace motivational speeches to the session you have with your psychologist, it is mentioned everywhere in abundance.

So, knowing that you have encountered this word countless times before, we expect you to wonder what exactly self-esteem is. We know the meaning of both these words on their own, but how do you define them when both these words are combined to form one phrase.

Before we can start talking about self-esteem and doing something about your self-esteem, you need to understand the concept of this word and how it came out to be as important as it is the world of psychology and motivation as it is today.

The basics of self-esteem can be understood by understanding the characteristics of people who have high self-esteem. High self-esteem can be said to be an abundance of respect and esteem for oneself in your mind.

People with high self-esteem are more often than not good friends with themselves. They enjoy their own company and accept themselves for who they are. They look after themselves and hold no bars in befriending their minds. You may know someone who looks after themselves, is intrinsically motivated and also happens to be quite a charmer when it comes to talking with other people. That someone probably has a good self-esteem, because they value themselves for who or what they are and do not mind talking to other people based on the face value that they have achieved over time. People with high self-esteem often happen to be intrinsically motivated as well.

If your biggest friend is present within you, you do not have to look at the outside world for motivation to do stuff. The biggest motivator present within you can help intrinsically motivate you to do stuff that you never imagined you would do. People with high self-esteem also offer amazing company. They can talk at ends about anything concerning life or them and do not hold any bars when it comes to expressing their desires.

On the other hand, we also expect you to know people or women who don't take care of themselves and don't have a heightened or realistic opinion of their abilities. They undermine their abilities, run into a lot of comparisons and do not actually realize how talented they are. In short, the kind of person we are talking of here would look in the mirror and hate themselves. Now, low self-esteem does not come down to ground facts or realities. Someone with low self-esteem could be the most beautiful woman alive with charming skin and whatnot, but their low self-esteem would prompt them into hating what they see in the mirror. Their bodies would never satisfy them, and they would almost always remain unfulfilled or unsatisfied with what they have given by good. It is believed that people with low self-esteem never end up achieving their true potential or what they truly can because they never realize all the talents that are hidden inside of them.

1. Overthinking

What is Overthinking?

T he mind is our more precious tool. But what happens when our thoughts start to get out of control? Humans are gifted with a superior thinking capacity that sets us apart from other living beings on this planet. The human brain can create great things like buildings, literature, movies, novels, and thousands of other inventions that have enhanced our way of life throughout history. It is remarkable what we can do when we put our minds to it.

Thinking allows us to excel in school, go to college, plan for the future, and get a job. No doubt, our mind is our biggest asset, but what happens when the mind stops being your ally and starts becoming your enemy? What if your mind starts to get out of control and starts eating away at your happiness? What would happen if your mind started producing destructive thoughts that threaten to hold you back in life and ruin the relationships you've worked so hard to build?

Overthinking Explained

Thinking too much. That is exactly what it means to overthink. When you spend too much time thinking instead of taking action, when you analyze and repeat the same thoughts in your mind but do very little about it, you're overthinking.

Or how about another, more relatable example of overthinking happening in a relationship. You send a text to your crush whom you've recently started dating. You wait eagerly for their reply, but an hour passes. Two hours. Three hours. Still nothing from them. Your mind starts to go into overdrive. Why aren't they texting me back? Are they busy? Have they lost interest in me? Was it something I said? Maybe they're annoyed that I'm texting them first. Maybe they want to break up with me. Could they be ghosting me? Is it me? Why does this always happen to me?

The Reason Behind It

To be trapped by the thoughts in your mind is torture. Being locked in and unable to escape the negativity is mental torture. The brain is tricky in that way. Telling it not think about something rarely ever works. We naturally want certainty. We want control. We want to know what's happening. We want concrete answers to the questions we have. When we don't get what we need to satisfy that urge, the brain goes into overdrive, coming up with scenarios of its own.

Why does overthinking happen? Well, along with the ability to think, humans have another special ability called intuition. Intuition is defined as the ability to immediately understand something without any need for conscious reasoning. Have you ever been told to "go with your gut" when you were stuck on a decision that had to be made? "Gut" in this context refers to your intuition, and it does highlight the fact that your intuitive thoughts are not coming from your conscious mind. Instead, they stem from your subconscious mind. If you've ever experienced those moments when it feels like your brain is arguing with itself, this is the reason why.

Your subconscious mind sometimes tries to give you answers to the problems you're facing. You need to make decisions every day. What makes it scary for a lot of people is how those decisions determine the direction your life is going and what you're going to experience next. This can be an overwhelming notion for many and why overthinking is such a problem. We're afraid of regret, and since time continues to move forward instead of backward, it feels like every decision that is going to impact our life matters. Once a decision has been made, you cannot go back in time and change the moment. You can't alter the choice you've made most of the time, and you must live with the consequences of your decisions. The last thing we want is to make a decision that we come to regret. We don't want to live with the possibility that we could have experienced something better if only we had made a different decision. See why overthinking is a big problem?

Ask anyone you meet, and they'll tell you that they don't want to look back on their life with regret when they're old one day, wishing they had done certain things differently. To complicate matters more, we never know what the guaranteed outcome is going to be for most of the decisions we make. Overthinking happens because the mind is constantly wrestling with the many possibilities it is faced with. The uncertainty of not knowing which decision is going to be the best decision only makes it harder to figure out the right choices to make.

Ultimately, the root cause of overthinking is fear. The seeds that it sows in your mind will prey upon your thoughts to the point they become out of control. None of us came into this world being afraid. The fear we experience today is what we've developed out of trauma or life experiences. Even when the traumatic experience has passed, remnants of that fear remain, and we continue to carry that fear around with us for the rest of our lives. Fear is the poison that latches unto our mind and, if left unchecked, triggers a lot of the overthinking that happens. These destructive thought patterns become an inescapable habit once it starts. The more we overthink, the more fear we invite in. The more fear we invite in, the more unsettled our thoughts are. It takes considerable effort to break out of this cycle and without the right support and tools to do it, it can feel nearly impossible to do.

The Dangerous Effects of Overthinking

Overthinking is a dangerous and unhealthy habit that needs to be broken. It will do nothing for you except to consume your energy and suck the happiness from your life. It puts a halt in your ability to make effective decisions, and you end up wasting a lot of time and energy being stuck in your head instead of taking proactive measures to create the outcomes you want. It's a habit that will leave you stagnant, sort of like tying a rope around your leg, and at the other end of the rope is a pole. Instead of moving forward, you find yourself running in circles around the pole, going nowhere fast.

Overthinking is the root of several problems, one of which is that it leads to an increased risk of developing mental illness. Some of these problems include:

- It Causes Mental Illness - According to a study conducted in 2013, that was published in the Journal of Abnormal Psychology, overthinking can lead to an increased risk of developing mental health problems (if you weren't dealing with these already). Ruminating traps you in a vicious negative cycle that can be extremely difficult to break out of if you don't have the right support and tools at your disposal. The unhappier you feel, the more your mental health declines, which eventually leads to some of the mental health problems talked about below.

- It Causes Anxiety - Your thoughts create emotions. It could be anything from grief, anger, sadness, happiness, joy, jubilation, eagerness, nervousness, and more. These are the sensations produced by thought. Anxious people are known to be overthinkers. They create so many possible scenarios in their minds about all the bad things that could possibly happen that they find themselves constantly plagued by anxiety. They worry about the future, and that stops them from living freely in the present. Living with so much anxiety each day makes them miserable, exhausted, and in more dire circumstances, it could lead to depression and suicidal thoughts. Yes, it is quite possible to literally think yourself to death.

- It Causes Depression - Anxiety comes from worrying about the future, while depression is a consequence of holding on to the past. Your thoughts keep you trapped in the events that have already happened, even though there's nothing you can do to change it now. However, overthinking is just one of the many possible causes of depression, and it is not solely responsible for this condition alone. Thinking about past events repeatedly wishing you could go back in time or change it will only make you miserable. Because there's no way to go back in time. Yet, some people continue to allow thoughts of the past to be a heavy burden that they carry with them every waking moment, leading to their feelings of unhappiness so strong it becomes depression. They waste precious time almost every day thinking about the "what if's" and wondering what would have happened if things had gone differently. "What if" is a question that weighs heavily on their mind and each time they think about it, they only become more miserable. The past cannot be changed, and the best you can do is to take the lessons from experience and use them for the benefit of your future to make better decisions. Like anxiety, depression can eventually lead to suicidal thoughts if your thoughts get the better of you.

- It Causes Insomnia - Does your worrying brain keep you awake all night long? Tossing and turning, you try to go to sleep, but the minute you close your eyes, your mind goes right back to whatever it is you were worrying about. Overthinking causes insomnia and even when your body may be tired, your mind remains active enough to keep you awake because your worried thoughts just won't leave you alone. Forcing yourself to go to sleep is not going to work either. Falling asleep is a mechanism that your mind cannot control and if your mind is too busy overthinking to shut down properly for the night, you'll be left to deal with insomnia. Trouble falling asleep is not something to be taken lightly. Sleep is essential for our overall well-being. To function at our best each day, we need to get enough sleep every night. To get the proper sleep, our bodies need each night; the mind needs to be fully relaxed, which you can't do if your mind is consumed by an unending stream of thoughts.

Your thoughts are powerful. They create the experiences that you have, and each time you overthink, you're sabotaging your happiness and wellbeing. If you've tried to forcibly control your thoughts before this, you probably haven't had much luck. The more you try to forcibly control your mind, the more resistance it seems to give. That's why overcoming negativity feels like such a struggle. Your mind is resisting because it is biased toward the negative, and it wants to stay in that zone where it feels comfortable. But when you observe your thoughts rather than try to control them, they'll automatically start to slow down as they pass in and out of your mind. Overcoming the habit of overthinking is not about forcing control; it is about understanding and acknowledgment. To understand what you're up against, acknowledge its presence and try to find a workable solution without trying to force control, that's when you're one step closer to becoming the master of your mind.

2. Symptoms of an Overthinker

N ow that you have an idea of what overthinking is, the following thing that you need to know is the signs of overthinking to look out for. Knowing the symptoms will inform you that you might need to be wary of the status of your mental health, maybe consider getting professional help. You can somehow gauge how deep into overthinking you are by identifying which symptoms have already manifested; if you find that you have signs of being a chronic overthinker, then you should probably consider getting professional help.

You Have Trouble Getting to Sleep

You cannot turn off your thoughts, even when you try; in fact, your thoughts actually start racing even faster when you try to stop them. All of these worries and doubts swirling in your head agitates you and prevents you from getting enough rest.

Overthinkers know the feeling of not getting enough sleep, almost too well actually. Insomnia happens because you have no control over your brain, you cannot shut off the chain of negative thoughts going through your mind at a hundred miles an hour. All of the things that worried you throughout the day comes back just when you hit the sack, and you feel so wired that you cannot fall asleep.

If you are having a hard time calming your mind on your own, you can try different relaxing activities before you go to bed. There are plenty of things that might help you ease your mind just enough to let you get some sleep, like meditation, writing on a journal, adult coloring books, drawing, painting, reading a book, or even just having a nice conversation with a loved one. Do anything that can shift your attention away from the negative thoughts long enough for you to get some sleep.

You Start to Self-Medicate

Numerous medical researchers have discovered that most people suffering from overthinking disorder have turned to using recreational drugs, alcohol, overeating, or other ways to somehow get a grip on their emotions. Overthinkers feel the need to rely on external stimuli because they believe that their internal resources (aka their minds) are already compromised.

It is never a good idea to turn to try to treat yourself from overthinking. Odds are, you will still be overthinking afterwards, and you have to deal with a different problem brought about by your self-medication.

You are Always Tired

If you are constantly feeling tired, you need to take action. Fatigue is your body's way of telling you to listen to it because there is something wrong going on; you should not ignore it and just hop from one activity to the other.

Usually, fatigue is caused by physical overexertion and lack of rest. However, overthinking can also cause fatigue and exhaustion. Your mind is like a muscle; if you are constantly burdening it with dozens of heavy, negative thoughts all the time, and not even giving it some time to recover, it will get exhausted and cause you to burn out.

Back when humans were still living off the land, people did not have that many things to worry about, which means they do not have quite as many things to think about as well. In today's modern world, people lead complicated lives that require them to accomplish a lot of things in a short amount of time. In this fast-paced world, the need to slow down every once in a while, is crucial for people's well-being. So, whenever you feel fatigued, or better yet, if you feel close to it, slow things down and figure out what your body, and your mind, needs before doing anything else.

You Tend to Overanalyze Everything

Overthinkers have one major problem, and that is that they always feel that they need to be in control of everything. They plan out every aspect of their lives, some of them even go as far as planning up to the smallest detail. They feel that doing this is the only way they can feel safe, but it always seems to backfire at them because it is actually impossible to plan for everything that will happen in their lives.

Even so, they still continue to plan out their futures, and they get anxious when unexpected things happen; and there always seem to be unexpected things happening all the time. Overthinkers hate dealing with things that they do not have control over, they fear the unknown. When unexpected problems do surface, they cause them to sit and mull things over instead of taking immediate action to solve the unexpected problem. Numerous medical studies have shown that overthinking leads to making poor judgment calls, which is why overthinking does not really help.

When you catch yourself just before you start overthinking, try your best to bring your thoughts back to the present by taking deep breaths and thinking happy thoughts. Before your negative thoughts go rampant inside your head, acknowledge them, and think about what they can do for you presently; doing this alone is usually enough to get rid of these negative thoughts, because you will discover that their only purpose is to cause you stress.

You are Afraid of Failure

You fancy yourself a perfectionist, and you often think about how awful you would feel if you were to somehow fail. This fear of failure can be so strong that it paralyzes you, and it keeps you from learning from your prior mistakes, which often lead to you repeating them.

Overthinkers often cannot accept failure, and they will do everything they can to avoid it. Ironically, they think that the only way to not fail is to do nothing at all. They mistakenly believe that in order to avoid failure, they should not put themselves in a position to fail at all, which also means they are not in the position to succeed as well. If this sounds like you, remember that you are more than just your failures; no one could even remember the last time that you screwed up, it's just you. Also, keep in mind that it is impossible to escape failure, and you should never avoid it at all. For failure allows you to grow and evolve.

You are Afraid of What the Future Holds

Instead of being excited of the things that you are yet to experience, your anxiety and fear of what could go wrong paralyzes you into doing nothing. If you are afraid of what the future could bring, then your fear keeps you trapped inside your own mind. Research shows that this fear of the future can be so crippling that sufferers tend to turn to drugs and/or alcohol just so they can tune out the negative thoughts that are clamoring inside their heads.

You Don't Trust Your Own Judgment

You cannot help yourself from second-guessing all of your decisions; from your outfit, what you will be having for lunch, or even what you will be doing for the day. You are always afraid that you will be making the wrong choices, and you often rely on others to reassure you that you made the right call.

Overthinkers, as mentioned earlier, are natural perfectionists; they constantly analyze, re-analyze, and re-analyze again, all situations that they find themselves in. They do not want to put themselves in a position where there is even a slight chance of failure. They do not want to make the wrong choice, so they take their sweet time making up their mind; they do not trust themselves enough to make the right decision for anything. They are so out of touch from their intuition that all of their decisions come from their brain, and this is not always right as there are times when you just need to follow your gut instinct. In addition, if your brain is bogged down from dozens of negative thoughts, it is hard to make a clear decision.

You Suffer from Frequent Tension Headaches

Tension headaches feel as if there is a thick rubber band wrapped around your temples, and it is slowly getting tighter. Aside from headache, you might also feel a sharp pain or stiffness in your neck. If you suffer from chronic tension headaches, it is a sign that you are overworking yourself and you need a rest.

And by rest, it also includes rest from mental activities, like overthinking. Headaches is a sign that your body needs to take a break, this includes your mind. In addition, you might not notice it, but when you overthink, you are actually thinking of the same things over and over again.

Overthinkers usually have negative thought patterns that loop around themselves. To fight this, you need to break this loop by reinforcing positive thoughts. Take deep breaths and focus your mind on every time your chest rises and falls, being mindful of the present will help you get rid of negative thoughts and the tension headache that came with them.

Signs You Are an Overthinker

- Chronic fatigue. The brain is at its maximum capacity when overthinking takes hold of your attention. Since the brain is a power-hungry organ system, it consumes a great deal of your usual energy. Hence, you may find yourself constantly tired bordering on exhaustion. This is why you often need more sleep than most folks.

- Overanalyzing everything. The chronic overthinkers make something out of everything. Even when someone makes a very innocent comment, the overthinker will find something and blow it out of proportion. Often, it is just a ploy to get the attention they crave.

- Dread of disappointment. The knit-picking tendencies of the overthinker lead them to constant disappointment. Since it is virtually impossible for them to take anything at face value, they will try to find the catch in everything. This leads to constant disappointment.

- Failure to be in the now. The overthinker is generally concerned about the past and focused on the future. This leads them to forget about living in the present that is, enjoying life's most precious moments, and the people around them.

- Continually re-thinking themselves. In other words, the overthinker is constantly second-guessing themselves, making unreasonable criticisms about themselves and the things they have done or failed to.

- Constant headaches. Given the fact that the brain is at full blast, the overthinker is generally prone to headaches. It is only when these folks are able to calm down that they find peace and solace in the world around them.

- Chronic sleeping disorders. Since overthinkers are prone to insomnia, they tend to be sleep deprived until their bodies shut down. At that point that they may oversleep as the body attempts to gain precious rest.

- Stiff muscles and joints. A chronic overthinker is in a constant state of stress. This may lead to maintain a consistent state of stiffness in joints and muscles. Hence, aches and pains throughout the body are very common.

- Living in dread. There is the overwhelming sensation of impending doom no matter how cut and dry things may be. After all, there is always the possibility that something could go wrong regardless of how far-fetched it may be.

- If you can relate to these characteristics, then it would be a great idea to find a person in whom you can trust, who can listen to you, so that you can ventilate at least some of your feelings as often as you can.

3. What are Stress and Anxiety ?

Anxiety is a natural response to fear or danger and can keep people safe in certain situations. Some people, however, experience anxiety more severely than others. This can lead to anxiety disorders, which can cause people to make major changes in their lives and habits to avoid situations or places that they believe cause them anxiety. If symptoms are persistent, a person might even be diagnosed with an anxiety disorder and recommended to seek treatment. Anxiety disorders can present themselves in a variety of ways; panic attacks, social anxiety, phobias, and separation anxiety to name a few.

A person might experience a host of physical symptoms with their anxiety, which can sometimes make it seem worse. Besides the unhealthy negative thoughts that are racing through their brain, they might also feel their heart racing, their temperature rising, or their breathing becoming shallower. These are all typical fight-or-flight responses that are triggered by anxiety to encourage a person to avoid the situation because the brain is perceiving it as a threat. It can be difficult for people to ignore thoughts of fear and dread when their body is pitching in and seemingly confirming them.

People experience anxiety for many different reasons, usually depending on their own life experiences and how their past has affected them. Some people have triggers for their anxiety, such as social situations or being separated from somewhere they feel is a safe space. Others feel anxiety in relation to nothing in particular but are constantly plagued with thoughts of fear and danger throughout the day. It can be difficult to deal with anxious feelings on a daily basis, but there are some things people can do to help ease the tension. This discusses the psychology of anxiety, common symptoms, potential triggers, and ways to find relief.

Anxiety Explained

Anxiety can be difficult for people to recognize when they are first experiencing it. Most people, in fact, might mistake it for a physical health problem due to the symptoms that accompany it. At its core, anxiety is a response to stress. It makes people feel scared or worried about certain situations for a variety of reasons. Some people might be worried that others will judge them for how they act or speak, others might be afraid that some harm will come to them if they put themselves in a certain situation. These feelings are not all abnormal, however. Some common anxiety-inducing situations include a child's first day of school, an initial job interview, or someone's wedding day. These experiences can all cause anxiety due to the uncertainty of the situation and might cause a person to start thinking about worst-case scenarios.

All of these feelings are part of anxiety because it was the evolutionary way of keeping people safe when their environment was inherently dangerous. The heightening of senses and increased heart rate prepares the body to run or fight if presented with danger, which could have meant life or death in prehistoric times. Today, however, people are not faced with imminent death on a daily basis, but their brain might not know how to adjust itself to the safety of modern life. It can still trigger anxious feelings if it is threatened to encourage a person to flee the situation, even if the reasons are not rational.

Some people experience anxiety to an extreme degree and can feel like their negative thoughts are unrelenting. For someone with this level of anxiety, quieting their mind and finding any kind of relief can be especially difficult and might even seem impossible. If a person suffers from anxiety of this intensity for an extended period of time, they might fit the criteria for an anxiety disorder. Typically, to qualify for a disorder diagnosis, a person has to experience symptoms for longer than six months or the symptoms need to be interfering with their daily life.

There are a variety of anxiety disorders that are all defined by how the anxiety affects someone or what causes anxious feelings. Each person is different, even though they might experience similar symptoms of anxiety, and the way their anxiety affects them can make a big difference in a diagnosis. Among these disorders is a plethora of negative side effects caused by the increased levels of stress and constant negative thoughts. Some people have trouble sleeping at night, have trouble concentrating during the day, find interacting with others especially difficult, or are too afraid to leave their own homes.

Some common anxiety disorders include panic disorder, phobias, social anxiety disorder, and separation anxiety. Obsessive-compulsive disorder is no longer considered an anxiety disorder, but people diagnosed with it often experience severe anxiety as one of their symptoms. Each of these common disorders associate anxiety with a particular object, situation, or action. These disorders can severely affect a person's life by making them unable to perform daily tasks or prevent them from enjoying their hobbies. For example, someone with agoraphobia—fear of crowds—may become so debilitated by fear that they refuse to leave their home.

The symptoms of anxiety are not necessarily universal and can vary greatly from person to person. Sometimes the reason a person has anxiety can determine their symptoms, as well. For example, someone who has anxiety because they think they are in danger might feel a pounding heart because their body wants to escape. Another person, however, who is dreading a social interaction, might experience an upset stomach due to the increased stress. Symptoms can range from gastrointestinal issues to cardiovascular discomfort, headaches, and in extreme cases even vomiting if stress builds up enough with the anxiety.

At the onset of symptoms, some people may suddenly feel like they are no longer in control of their body. This can often increase feelings of anxiety because they may not feel like the dread or physical symptoms will ever subside. Sometimes this out of control feeling can even lead to panic attacks. Other startling symptoms can include nightmares or constantly recalling painful thoughts or memories. These can also contribute to increased stress and anxiety because a person might feel like they cannot escape their own negative thoughts or what might seem to be an inevitably painful outcome of an event.

In people with generalized anxiety, it is more common to worry about things because of a past experience. For example, if a child's parent forgot them in a grocery store for an extended time, that child might then develop a fear of grocery stores and feel unsafe when they go to one. This could potentially carry on into adulthood, even if the person doesn't remember the event that instigated their anxiety. Common symptoms of this type of anxiety usually present themselves when a person is in a certain situation or sometimes if they merely consider putting themselves in the trigger situation. These people often experience a racing heart, shortness of breath or rapid breathing, restlessness, trouble focusing, and a slew of other symptoms.

Anxiety can even affect a person's stomach function, causing gas, constipation, or diarrhea when it flares up. This can also contribute to more severe anxiety in a person because they may become fixated on their stomach problems and convinced that if they are in a social situation, they might have a problem they cannot get away to handle. Some people can experience this discomfort even at the thought of doing something that gives them anxiety. This is why it can be particularly difficult for people to overcome their anxiety. If even the thought of doing something makes them feel physically ill, it can be difficult to convince themselves that actually doing it won't be painful.

When people experience these intense physical symptoms in relation to their anxiety, it can often cause them to start avoiding things, situations, or people that they believe will trigger their negative feelings. Although this might seem like an effective coping mechanism to those with anxiety, it can actually severely limit their lives by making them unable to participate in normal everyday tasks. On top of wanting to avoid these situations, anxiety can make a person feel too weak or fatigued to engage in social activities. This further cement their desire to withdraw and stay confined to their safe space instead of facing and managing their anxiety.

Causes and treatments

Most people feel anxious at some point in their life, but there can be certain factors or triggers that cause other people to feel it more severely than normal. These can include someone's genetics, their environment, how their brain is wired, and what life experiences they've had. If a person associates something with fear, it is likely they will develop anxiety surrounding that thing. Although it is typical for people to have some sort of trigger for their anxiety, this is not true for all cases. Some people have very generalized anxiety about nothing in particular; they are simply always worried or dreading being out in the world.

For some people, one type of anxiety can cause them to develop another type of anxiety. For example, someone who has anxiety about suffering harm or getting sick might develop a germ-related obsessive-compulsive disorder as a way to ensure they will never get sick. Or, people with social anxiety disorder might eventually develop agoraphobia if they never force themselves to interact with others.

Risk factors for different types of anxiety disorders typically coexist in people who suffer with them, which demonstrates that no single experience is likely to cause someone to develop a disorder. Scientists have found that nature and nurture are strongly linked when it comes to the likelihood that someone will develop severe anxiety. Genetically, research has shown that people have about a 30 to 67 percent chance of inheriting anxiety from their parents (Carter, n.d.). Although someone's DNA might be a factor in them developing anxiety, it cannot account for all of the reasons that have developed it.

Environmental factors should also be taken into consideration when trying to find the root cause of anxiety. Parenting style can be a large factor in whether or not a person will develop anxiety. If parents are controlling of their children or if they model anxious behaviors, the child might grow up thinking these are normal behaviors they should model. This can lead to feeling anxious based on a learned behavior. Other factors such as continual stress, abuse, or loss of a loved one can also elicit a severe anxious reaction because a person may not know how to handle the situation they find themselves in.

In addition to the environment, a person's health can often cause anxiety as well. If someone is diagnosed or living with a chronic medical condition or a severe illness, it can cause an anxious reaction. One possibility is if the illness is affecting the person's hormones which can cause stress, or if their feelings of not having control are worsened by a diagnosis they cannot fix.

Some people might not realize that the choices they make daily could be contributing to their anxiety. Things such as excessive caffeine, tobacco use, and not exercising enough can all cause anxiety. Caffeine and other stimulants can increase a person's heart rate and simulate anxiety symptoms. Not exercising can lower a person's level of happy hormones and make their muscles tense or sore which can also contribute to stress. A person's personality can also determine how severe their anxiety might be. Shy people who tend to stay away from conversations and interaction might develop more severe social anxiety because they are not exposed to those situations often.

When experiencing anxiety, it can seem like there is no way out, but there are actually quite a few different ways a person can work to ease their worries, ranging from clinical to holistic approaches. What type of treatments will work depends on the person, and often, how severe their struggle is.

A few clinical ways to treat anxiety include counseling, psychotherapy, and medication. These are not the only ways a person can be medically treated, but they tend to be the most conventional routes for treating mental illness. Counseling is a type of therapy where the person is able to talk to a licensed practitioner and receive feedback and advice about their situation and how to handle their emotions. Most counselors have a master's degree in the psychology field and are licensed through their state. This type of therapy is usually considered a short-term solution for people who are struggling but not debilitated by their anxiety.

Psychotherapy is typically a more long-term solution for people whose lives are impacted by their anxiety. This type of therapy can focus on a broader range of issues and triggers such as a person's anxious patterns or behaviors and how to fix them. Cognitive behavioral therapy is often used in this type of therapy to work with the person to adjust their thoughts and behaviors.

Some people find relief once prescribed medication to help them manage their anxiety. This route is usually reserved for people who are struggling the most and having trouble calming themselves on their own. There are various types of medications such as SSRIs (selective serotonin reuptake inhibitors) and SNRIs (serotonin-norepinephrine reuptake inhibitors) that alter brain chemicals to reduce anxiety or worry.

Making changes to their lifestyle and habits can also help people with anxiety relieve some of their symptoms. This is a more natural approach to managing anxiety and can be successful for people who are dedicated to making positive life changes. Small things such as diet adjustments and increasing activity levels can reduce anxious feelings. Establishing a consistent sleep schedule is also important to help someone ensure they are getting enough rest each night. Stress fatigues the body and it may need more time to fully recuperate at night if it was taxed during the day. Making sure the body has a routine can also make someone feel safe and know what to expect from their day.

Meditation can also be a good way for people to calm their minds and ease anxiety. Taking time during the day to be still and quiet might help someone stop the constant worry they feel during the day and relax for a moment. Once they start training their body to relax, it is more likely that they can keep it up during the day. Finally, avoiding stimulants such as caffeine, sugar, and tobacco, and depressants such as alcohol can greatly improve a person's chances of overcoming their anxiety. These substances contribute to the brain's hyperactivity and can often increase feelings of anxiety.

Recognizing Stress: How to Calm your Body

Did you know that one-third of the United States population reported to experiencing extreme levels of stress? These statistics was obtained from a 2007 poll of the American Psychological Association. This was more than a decade ago. Now imagine what the percentage will be now with all that's going on in the free world. Stress has the tendency of making people feel overwhelmed with the goings-on around them. According to that poll, about one in every five persons reported that they experience high levels of stress not less than fifteen days in every month. Although it has been proved that low levels of stress do not pose any immediate threat to your health, but escalated and poorly managed stress can produce life threatening conditions. Your ability to recognize high stress levels and the stressors will help you know the exact ways to act promptly in the healthiest ways that will help you change unhealthy behaviors thereby regaining and maintaining control over your health. And for you to achieve this there are situations you must pay attention. Paying attention to those situations will help you understand your stress pattern, the stressors, and how you can avoid future occurrence.

You should be aware of your stress pattern

Being that everyone experiences stress differently and on different occasions, understanding how your stress occurs, what your stressors are and how you get to understand that you are stressed will go a long way in helping you maintaining calmness during and after a stressful episode. Also, your ability to understand how you react to stressful situations is also important. This concerns your thoughts and behavior and how they align with or react to your stressors and stress. When you understand this, you will be able to point out the difference in your behavior during the times you are stressed and the times when you're not.

You should identify the sources of your stress

Identifying the sources of your stress also means shooting the dart on your stressors. To do this effectively, you have to be more attentive to the moments before a stressful situation. The reason for the extra attention is for you to identify the particular events or situations that trigger stress feelings. Being able to do this will go a long way in helping you plan your life or change your lifestyle. For instance, if you discover that the relationship that exists between you and your family members, or between you and your employer or a colleague at work, or the relationship that exists between you and a neighbor is your stressor, what you do after this discovery will determine whether you deal with stress and maintain good health, or whether these stressors will continue to haunt you at the expense of your health.

There is also the possibility of your stressor arising from financial predicaments or decisions. It could be from much workload or the lack of a job. It could be from the consequences of a bad decision. Whatever you identify as your stressor, you should know that taking steps to avoid or discontinue their activities in your life will help you calm your body.

4. Declutter Your Mind To Clean Your Thoughts

What is Decluttering?

Decluttering means to remove things from that you no longer need from a place to make it more useful and pleasant.

Importance of Decluttering for Self-care:

It might not seem at first as if decluttering your house has much to do with self-care. Yet I learned that not only is your home being decluttered a form of self-care practice. But to self-care is essential to declutter. Actually, very important!

What is Self-Care?

Self-care is behavior that we adopt to protect and improve our own health, well-being, and happiness. While many of us have a concept of bubble baths, manicures, and massages as self-care activities, it really involves a lot more than that.

Indeed, self-care is not just fun things like bubble baths and manicures (though those are definitely ways you can take care of yourself!). Self-care also involves doing things that improve your life, wealth, safety, and/or happiness (sometimes hard things or stuff you don't really want to do).

For example, self-care can also mean having your doctor check an annual checkup. Or floss your teeth every night, exercise even during the days you don't like it, or go to bed instead of staying up to watch another episode.

And sometimes, self-care involves things that you don't even consider to be self-care, like decluttering! But decluttering is not only a way to practice self-care, but it is necessary for self-care to declutter.

Negative impact of clutter in our lives:

While when we're in the middle of it, we may not always realize that clutter can have a really negative effect on our life.

How much of the clutter that steals from us in our home? Our time, our space, and our energy definitely. But also, it can take our peace.

Clutter and stress:

Too much "stuff" and clutter can, in a variety of ways, cause considerable stress in your life. Here are a few examples: it takes a lot more time to keep up with housework, and effort in a cluttered home. More stuff depicts more stuff to make a mess with and more time and energy to clean up those messes. It's very hard to keep track of what you own, causing you to spend a plenty of time looking for stuff or even buying items because you can't find it. Feeling discontent with the condition of your home can cause stress and even embarrassment to host guests.

Clutter and well-being:

Not only this, but too much clutter can also change how you feel at home and how your home affects your well-being.

Clutter can often cause you to feel unhappy about your home and depressed in general.

Most of us want to make our home a place to which we can retreat and relax. But a cluttered home can make it challenging to rest and relax.

You're not just constantly bombarded with visual clutter, distractions, and "things." Which never gives white spaces for your mind and eyes to rest on.

But too much stuff to handle can also make you feel like you're to-dodo list is endless. Or as if there is always more to do to keep your home, and you cannot keep up or catch up.

When there's a room full of clutter and "things," it often doesn't feel calm, soothing, or happy. And might even go as far as adding a considerable amount of anxiety to your life.

Decluttering is important to self-care On the other hand, it can have a really positive impact on your life and well-being, to clear the clutter and remove the excess and distractions from home.

In so many ways decluttering is freeing. To get rid of the excessive amount of "useless things" that fills your home often feels like a lifting weight from your life.

We don't even know sometimes how heavy and burdensome our stuff makes us feel before we start letting it go! And once you're starting to let go, it can feel like such a big relief as you feel lighter and happier and start experiencing less benefits.

The decluttering provides other practical benefits. For starters, you'll be spending less time and energy cleaning and keeping a clean house. And you'll probably lose less of your keys!

Nevertheless, decluttering is essential for self-care because there are also many intangible benefits. Clearing the clutter can impact your overall health, happiness, and well-being so positively.

Self-care benefits of decluttering:

Here are a few scenarios which explain how decluttering is important to self-care

By improving your overall well-being and quality of life:

Clearing the clutter literally means giving yourself more space in your home. And more space means you create white space and breathing room in your home. It facilitates rest and relaxation.

Nonetheless, more space in your home can make you happier at home.

Instead of feeling unhappy with your home, and wishing you had a bigger house, owning less might make you realize that you don't need a bigger home, just less stuff!

More time:

You have less "stuff" to manage when you own less. You spend less time cleaning, cleaning, and caring for the things that you own, simply because there is less.

Then you get more time for what matters to you most. It could be more time spent with the people you love. Got more time for an activity that you love. Or more time for whatever is important to you!

Whatever it is, you will have more time to spend on what you value most once your home and the things you own require less of your time to maintain them.

More energy:

Just like fewer stuff means less time to manage it. Also, less stuff means less energy needed to achieve it. You will then have more energy and attention to dedicate to what matters most to you.

More presence:

It is easier to be more present and less distracted when you have less stuff stealing your time, energy, and attention.

More money:

If you're working hard to declutter your home, the last thing you want to do is fill it up with more things. Choosing to own less often results in choosing less to buy, which can save your money!

And anything that we can do to relieve stress around money is great for our self-care.

More focus:

Clearing the clutter means less of managing the "stuff" you own is taken on your mental capacity. You have less fatigue in making decisions, simply because you own fewer things, and you have less to decide about.

When all of the "things" and noise around you are not continuously distracting your brain, you have more ability to focus and concentrate.

Removing the physical clutter from home can also help clear the mental clutter, as you're to-dodo list shrinks, and the distractions diminish.

More peace:

Maintaining your home is less stressful when your home takes less time and energy. Not only that, but it's easier to keep your home clean so you can rest, relax and enjoy more of your life.

This all leads to greater feelings of happiness and peace. Along with making your house more contented.

More freedom:

You give yourself the independence to build a life you love when you have more time, space, and energy.

So much "things" will no longer weigh you down and stress you. Instead, you get the chance to fill your life with what matters most to you.

Owning less is not about deprivation:

We often buy stuff to make life more enjoyable or more comfortable. But too much of a good thing can turn out to be wrong.

Too much stuff stops making our lives easier and starts adding a burden to our lives. The more we own, the more we have to work to pay for, collect, clean, maintain, organize, search, repair, etc. It's not about depriving yourself of things you love or things that make life easier. Probably just the same!

Decluttering and simplifying are about getting rid of the clutter, the excess, and the distractions, so you have more time, space, energy, and freedom in your life for what matters most to you.

Be careful to be at your best. That may not be the case for you. You can ignore the messes and clutter and stay with your family.

But if clutter and mess cause you to feel stressed, cranky, or incapable of feeling present, maybe decluttering is important for you too. The point is, how good you are as a mom or how happy your children are having nothing to do with how clean your floors and oven are, or not.

And it is all concerned with how well you take care of yourself as a person so that you and your family can be at their best.

And it just happens that decluttering is one way you can simplify your life to take care of yourself and to be a better mother or father.

Decluttering can become a meaningful way to practice self-care because it helps you take control of your home, life, and "stuff" to improve your overall well-being.

These are just a few of the reasons why it is important to declutter for self-care. If you are struggling to get motivated to declutter, try to remind yourself that it is about so much more than a clean home to clear the clutter.

It's also about having a house where you can fill up rather than deplete. Create a home that can give you time, space, energy, and clarity to improve your overall health, happiness, and well-being!

Ways to Organize Thoughts:

In an increasingly jumbled mess, everything is swirling about, and you don't seem to make sense of anything.

There are, happily, ways to catch all those fun little ideas.

- Practical ways to organize your thoughts

- Using sticky notes and a frame.

- Take a stack of sticky notes and sit near a wall or stand. Write down one thought per sticky note, then hang the note on the wall. Continue until you have a bunch of notes; then begin sorting the notes into groups by hand.

Draw the Mind Map

A mind map is a way of bringing together different thoughts. Begin by drawing a single thought from a piece of paper in the middle. Instead, draw a line out of that thought, radiating outward to the edge of the page, adding a similar or related thought. Continue to add thoughts to your map, ensuring things are connected to each other.

Take Notes on Your Index Card:

Index cards are a great way to track your ideas and thoughts. For a primary thought, you can use the top red line and list similar thoughts below on each of the following lines, or you can use a single card for a thought or concept. Shuffle your cards as you look for new ways of sorting and organizing information.

Create A List:

Record a good old-fashioned list of your feelings. Keep one thought to a line, and keep going until all of your thoughts are written down for the moment. You can then go back and start sorting the list into smaller items.

Here's an easy way for you to hear what you actually think. Take a voice recorder or voice recording device to record your thoughts. Put the recording aside for a day or two, then come back and check it out. You're going to have another viewpoint on your feelings.

Thoughtful Ways to Organize Your Thoughts:

The next time boredom hits at home, try to tackle this list of productive tasks.

Do An Operation To Brain-Off?

It would help if you focused on something without thinking about it. This could be inputting business card data into spreadsheet, ironing clothing, sewing and knitting, dusting furniture, filing paper, or cleaning up your desk or room. Let your mind sort out the things as you go about working.

Rest, or meditate peacefully:

Meditation will relax both body and mind. It can also help you subconsciously work out those feelings. Draw the blinds, switch off the lights, or dim them, and sit on the floor or in a chair.

Sleep on it:

What now seems messy and confusing, in the morning, should look a lot different. If the thoughts in your head do not seem to make sense, go to sleep for the night.

PHYSICAL WAYS TO ORGANIZE YOUR FEELINGS

Get some Exercise:

Moving your body and beating your blood. Visiting the gym, running around, playing frisbee, or a game of catching with a friend, or walking and making any mistakes. Changing pace will give your mind a break, and let your subconscious work in the background on your puzzle.

Spend Time In Nature:

Go out and have a little outdoor time. You can sit on a bench in the park, walk a trail, walk your dog, or look at a lovely green pasture. Get out of your hearing and take your eyes in the sights.

Talk to a friend or any member of your family:

It does help to talk things out sometimes. You're going to feel better getting something out of your head, off your chest. Plus, your friend can surely help you find patterns you might miss, or clarify, and strengthen what you're thinking.

Tell a tale:

The process of telling a tale aloud will make you think about what is and what is not essential. So, Take a start with one of your thoughts and come up with a story. "It was a time"

SIMPLE STEPS TO BOOST YOUR BRAIN POWER:

Our brains are ordered, mainly, like human computers. They work in much the same way to a large extent. And if we want to boost our everyday productivity, we need to clear the temporary "data" cache and reboot our brains to allow us to perform at our peak levels.

Otherwise, we can quickly encounter brain overload with too many simultaneous circuits and so many programs (thought) running in the shadows that we often "freeze up." This will render us incapable of recalling everything or just processing the information less quickly than we would like.

It sounds odd, but it actually makes sense when you start to consider.

You will drastically improve your ability to focus, complete tasks, and achieve your goals by making it a routine to set aside a few minutes each day to clean and organize your brain.

A concentrated mind is far more successful than one, which is continuously overwhelmed.

Furthermore, a brain overwhelmed forgets things, important tasks, information, and deadlines. The product rate, too, is suffering. We obviously cannot focus and use our intellect and skills to their maximum potential.

You'll find better balance, less stress, and greater energy as a side benefit. Swirling thoughts cause enormous tension and are stopping our minds from ever fully resting. This leads to brain tiredness which makes us exhausted and irritable.

That's not really that hard to organize your thoughts. It really only takes a few minutes each day to help sharpen your brain with surprisingly simple tools. Here are three simple steps to boost your mega brainpower.

1.   Select the Best Time:

Ideally, this process is best done twice a day, first thing in the morning and again before bedtime, but it doesn't work for everyone.

Choose the time that suits you best. It'll work every time. The trick is being consistent in doing so.

Some people find morning coffee, breakfast, and workout required first. Because they think their brain must be waking up a little bit. They clearly need a boost in caffeine, a release of fuel, and tension to form coherent thoughts.

2.   Choose Your Logging Method:

Any sort of productivity or note-taking apps on your phone will work well for recording your thoughts and tasks. You can use the voice-recording option if you prefer. Even the role of base note works fine.

An organizing software or folder on your computer can function as well, such as Outlook, OneNote, or Evernote.

Though by nature, some tend to be a "techie," They still prefer using a pen and pad for that process. Often, the most effective method is the easiest.

Whatever tool you choose, make sure it is easily accessible and quick.

3. Quickly Dump Everything:

Dump everything you Have in your head and make sure everything... Not just jobs, but feelings, worries, questions, and ideas too.

Get them all out. Don't think about figuring them out that you can do later. Just get them out of your mind so they can stop spinning around, and use valuable brainpower and energy.

Ask yourself whether you need or want to act on any of those items today once you've done.

If the answer is yes: add or remove these tasks to your ongoing task or to-do list (do you have one of those rights?).

If no is the answer: Is that an idea? Add it to a file of ideas, a work notebook, or a document to follow up later on.

Is it really more of a problem you have, or concerns? –File it in a newspaper or notebook to then mull about. (If you never go back to look at them, maybe they weren't so important!) It's so easy. Not more than 5 to 10 minutes should be required!

5. Techniques of Guided Meditation To Quit Anxiety

Relaxation is an incredibly effective way of dealing with anxiety, and it applies to all groups of people. It allows the body to activate its natural response to combat stressors. Relaxation comes in many forms and depends on what works best for you. Some of the relaxation techniques that have been proven to beat back anxiety are:

· Relaxation exercises such as muscle relaxation and deep breathing

· Meditation

· Visualization

· Physical activities like yoga

There is a common belief among many people that relaxation involves sitting idle and or doing something you enjoy, like watching a movie or sleeping. No, relaxation is a task that needs concentration and energy input. Its sole purpose is to reduce the effects of stress and anxiety. If your definition of relaxation doesn't meet this goal, then it is far from relaxation. Relaxation achieves this by putting your body to a state of deep rest and restores normalcy such as slowing the heart rate, reducing blood pressure, improve blood circulation, and most importantly checking stress and anxiety. Activities that involve relaxation are those that touch on the most affected organs like the heart, blood vessels, and those in the breathing system. Try things like muscular exercises, meditation, yoga, and deep breathing. Most of these exercises are a form of self-treatment, so you don't need a professional to do them. However, they are quite demanding and require a lot of discipline. If you are the type that needs to be pushed, you might consider looking for a professional therapist to help you do the exercises. The word 'professional' is key because not anybody can make you do things that make you uncomfortable, especially if you're an adult. You need someone that will be hard and a little harsh on you. Also, people have diverse systems that respond differently to changes. If one or two of these exercises don't work for you, look for one that you are comfortable doing and is compatible with your system. You don't have to kill yourself trying to make a particular technique work even you can see that it is not working. Furthermore, all these techniques have been proven to lead to the same results, which is slowing down stress and anxiety. Just don't be too lazy to give a particular technique trial and error period before giving up on it entirely. Remember things take time; you need to give your body a chance to get used to these changes. You will get used to those exercises in no time, and they will become a habit.

There is a thin line between relaxation exercises and meditation exercises. The main difference being that relaxation exercises engage various parts of the physical body while meditation engages the brain. The similarity between them is that they both put the entire body and mind in a state of rest to relief affected parts and organs from stress and anxiety. Both exercises are carried out in systematic steps to the end. Skipping one step will likely jeopardize the whole process. If you are not sure about these steps and the order in which they are done, it is advisable that you seek the help of a therapist who will take you through each step.

Deep Breathing

This is the bedrock of all other relaxation exercises. It is the simplest yet very effective way of keeping your anxiety level in check. It communicates safety to the brain, thus easing tension, stress, and anxiety. It involves improving your breathing by cleansing and opening air cavities for normal breathing to occur. Anybody can do this without any difficulty. It doesn't matter where you do it, anywhere is a perfect place as long as the environment is conducive. Conducive means it is free from noise and particle pollution. There should also be minimal disruption from other people and things. Remember this is a procedure with its own timeline; if you are interrupted say in the third step, you won't resume the exercise from the third step. You will have to start all over again and make sure it goes to completion. This is the procedure:

Identify a quiet spot outdoors, say in the park, or lock yourself up in a clean well-ventilated room. You can also sit down on a chair with your feet touching the ground or lie down with your body straight against the ground or floor. Whatever position makes you feel comfortable.

Sit up straight with your legs straight against the floor or ground, spread them apart or fold them on the knees and let the back of your feet touch. Your back should not lean on anything. Your left hand should be on your abdomen and the right on the chest. Take a deep breathe through your nose for as long as you can, relax the hand on your abdomen to allow the stomach muscles to relax and accommodate more air.

Exhale through your mouth for as long as you can, lightly push your stomach in and contract the muscles to push all the air out.

Repeat this process for like five minutes non-stop. Minimize the movement of the arm on your chest. Focus only on your breathing and try to shut down your brain from all thoughts, whether positive or negative. Make sure the breathing is slow and smooth, don't try to increase the pace. Do this thrice day, each exercise should last at least five minutes, but you can go up to fifteen minutes if you like.

Progressive Muscle Relaxation

This is a two-step process of muscular contraction and relaxation involving various groups of muscles in the body. This exercise is important because it demonstrates how your body physically responds to stress and anxiety. Remember, this is a mental disorder that is not easy to detect, but if we incorporate physical aspects in detection, it will be much easier to know when we are experiencing anxiety. The exercise can be combined with deep breathing to yield maximum results. For you to carry out this exercise, you must be in your best form health-wise; no muscle spasms, no back pains or recent injuries that might put unnecessary strain on the muscles. In case you have or suspect to have any of these problems, consult your doctor before starting the exercise. Here is the procedure.

Put on some comfortable loose clothing or loosen the ones you are wearing by unbuttoning top buttons and sleeves. Remove belts and shoes.

Repeat the steps as those in deep breathe, do it once or twice in this step.

Look at your feet in turn, start with one and spend some seconds looking at it. Move your toes slowly and follow their movement and other induced movements within the foot. Squeeze the muscles as tightly as you can within the foot. Make sure the muscles are tense for some ten seconds before relaxing them. Notice the change and difference between the two exercises.

Repeat this for the other foot and focus on the movement and behavior of the muscles as you squeeze them, and when you relax them.

Notice what tension does to your feet. You can do this by comparing how the foot feels when in tension and when relaxed.

Shift your attention to other groups in your body, such as the hand muscles, stomach muscles, and neck and shoulder muscles. Repeat the process for each and pay attention. Notice the kind feeling associated with tensing various groups of muscles.

Relaxation by Visualizing

This technique involves playing games with the brain by showing it what it desires. It is a very effective technique to combat anxiety because it gives you temporary peace and calmness. You can cultivate this good feeling by repeating this exercise for as many times as possible until it sticks.

If you feel like you're experiencing anxiety, find a quiet place, and make yourself comfortable. You can sit or stand against something like a wall.

Close your eyes, think of your ideal space — a place you would like to be in the real world or just an imaginary one.

Imagine the life there, the feeling, smell of things there, and their sounds. Think about the people you would find in that place and how awesome they are. Let that picture stick in your mind.

Open your eyes and take a deep breathe, severally. Try to feel your mind and notice if you are still experiencing anxiety.

If the anxiety tries to crawl back again, close your eyes once more and retrieve the picture of your ideal place from your mind and go back there. Experience the peace, calmness, and comfort associated with that place for as long as you can.

Repeat this process every time you feel anxious and notice if there are any changes in the completion of the exercise. Remember that the effectiveness of the procedure is determined by the amount of time you give the body to process the change. It never comes that easy, so be patient.

Relaxation through Yoga

Yoga is a workout trend that has taken the world by storm in the last ten years. It combines a series of moving and stationary poses. It also involves meditation, and this makes it an all-round relaxation technique. Apart from increasing stability, stability, and general fitness, yoga is also a powerful weapon to fight anxiety. The following different types of yoga deal with different bodily and mental problems.

Satyananda yoga- this traditional form of yoga is usually considered to be the original yoga. It is centered on meditation though it also incorporates slow poses and deep breathing. This gives it an incredible ability to combat anxiety and other psychological disorders. It is the easiest type of yoga if you are a beginner.

Hatha yoga- this type of yoga involves moderate poses and movements. After mastering all aspects of Satyananda yoga, hatha yoga is the next step to sharpen your yoga skills and improve your ability to keep anxiety at bay.

Power yoga- this is the most intense type of yoga; we can say it is a reserve of the pros. However, this intense pose gives you the ability to deal with intense stress.

Tai chi- most authors don't consider this a type of yoga, but there is a strong reason to classify it as yoga. It involves moving your body in a slow, systematic pattern and accompany it with slow but deep breathing. It is a powerful relaxation method to relieve stress and anxiety.

Like we have seen earlier, meditation is more of a psychological approach to combat anxiety. It involves freeing your mind to choose thoughts with the hope that this will serve as a counter-trigger. There are two main types of meditation.

Mindfulness Meditation

The effectiveness of this method has been put to the test by therapists, physicians, and psychologists for the last two decades. The results have been quite impressive, and it has since been used as a tool to relieve the mind from stress and anxiety. How exactly this method works is still a mystery, but it remains a powerful anxiety therapy method. Some authors have suggested that it works by confining the brain to the present, and by doing that it shuts down traumatic memories and uncertainties of the future. This makes a lot of sense because most stresses are caused by trauma and fear of what might happen. By eliminating these two, the brain can then focus only on current events. Events that deal with reality, free of perceived threats. This is how to practice mindfulness:

Repeat all the steps as with deep breathing above. Focus on your breathe alone, follow every inhalation and exhalation for as long as you can.

Monitor your mind as you focus on your breathing. Try to notice when your thoughts are about to wander and try to follow them. Notice the sounds, smells, and types of worries that your mind picks, then try to bring them back by going back to focusing on your breathing.

Allow your mind to wander once more, not anything particular, but to anything it wants. Let this wandering go on for a while then bring it back again by focusing on your breathing.

Repeat the process for about 10 minutes, twice a day or five times a week. Notice if there is any change in the level of anxiety from when you started the exercise.

Body Scan Meditation

This technique is almost similar to progressive muscle relaxation. The only difference is that it involves listening to the reaction of other parts of the body to muscular movement without judgment. This is the procedure for body scan meditation.

Lie on your back, relax your hands on your sides and keep your legs straight or crossed. Close your eyes and take a deep breathe through the nose and exhale through the mouth. Follow your breathing for like five minutes.

Shift your focus to your feet, contract the muscles of the right foot, and notice the movement of the toes. Feel the effect this tension on the muscles has on different parts of the body as you tense them even tighter.

Repeat this process for the left foot and feel the tension in other regions.

Move to a different body part, say your thighs, and repeat this process. Try noticing the impact this tension has on other parts of the body. Keep moving to your knees, calf, torso, abdomen until you have scanned every part.

After you are done, sit in stillness and quietness and try to remember what you felt in different parts and organs during the exercise.

Repeat this procedure twice or thrice a day and notice the changes in your level of anxiety.

Benefits of Relaxation Techniques

All these techniques have a wide range of benefits both to the body and to the mind. Apart from the benefit of managing anxiety, relaxation techniques are helpful in various other areas as follows:

Improved breathing- techniques that involve deep breathing like meditation and yoga play an important role in opening up air pipes and facilitating the free flow of clean air in and out of the system. Even if one experiences anxiety, chances are that their breathing system will not be harmed.

Mental stability- these exercises and techniques do not only curb anxiety, but they also prevent many other psychological and mental disorders, so you are actually killing two birds with one stone. This is made possible when you keep your mind busy and divert it from the cause of anxiety. This diversion applies to other underlying conditions of the mind.

Spices up one's social life- most of these relaxation activities and techniques are done in groups such as yoga classes and Tai chi. They expose one to different kinds of people and actually make them more sociable. Once someone starts socializing with others, the chances are that they will talk about their problems and get help.

Boosts confidence- anxiety becomes worse if the affected individual considers themselves weak. As soon as these exercises start gaining momentum, you will notice a feeling of self-pride and confidence running through you. This is a hidden benefit of applying these relaxation techniques.

Engages the brain- most people would actually use their free time to worry about ambiguous threats. This will only increase their chances of developing anxiety. Participating in these relaxation exercises will engage the brain, and you won't be thinking about some imaginary threats and problems. By the time you are done with the exercise, it will be time to resume your normal duties, and this keeps your too brain busy to indulge in unhealthy thinking.

Keep in mind that not everyone responds well to anxiety exercises and relaxation techniques. The symptoms may actually worsen for some people. If you notice that these exercises are not doing you any good, go see a doctor immediately for further direction. Seeking professional help is important since you might be suffering from other hidden illnesses.

Explanation of the Reference Technique

This is a technique that attempts to divert the mind from a perceived threat or source of anxiety by shutting down most body reflexes that receive, process, and respond to these threats. It is very effective in offering self-therapy when dealing with anxiety and other psychological disorders. The reference technique follows the following steps.

Find a comfortable and quiet place, and sit down, close your eyes.

Think of things that follow a chronological order like numbers, letters of the alphabet, months, or days. Start counting from the start to the end. Start counting again but this time in the opposite direction, from the last to the first.

Focus attention on various parts of the body as you do the counting. Notice if there is some reducing tension in some groups of muscles like those in the abdomen, back, and neck. Don't stop counting as you do the listening.

Suspend all muscular activities by turning off the muscles. Don't tense or relax them; just stay still, and focus on your counting.

Release your mind to think about anything, give it the freedom to wander from one thought to another, including your worries. Don't try and stop it if it tries to think about unpleasant things. Just listen and view the pictures without being judgmental.

After allowing your mind to wander on all kinds of thoughts, now start sorting out those thoughts. Removing all negative thoughts, those that you consider unpleasant and makes you worried. Only remain with positive thoughts and statements that make you feel safe and peaceful. Reflect on these positive thoughts for like two minutes.

Open your eyes, take a deep breath, and reflect on the feeling you have just experienced before opening your eyes.

Repeat this for some two times every day and notice whether your level of anxiety is changing from the first day.

6. Meditative Breathing Techniques

While there are multiple meditative breathing processes and practicing, for the purposes of this brief guide, we will be concentrating on five specific techniques that allow you to better induce meditative focus; they are Shamantha, Nadi Shondhana, Zuanqi, Khumbaka Pranayama and Box Breathing.

Shamantha is a Buddhist breathing technique that teaches you to breathe in your natural rhythm. Generally, Shamantha breathing is known as the "reset breathing" technique, because it is meant to help you come back to the present moment. In order to practice Shamantha breathing you need to first relax your body, and stretch out your spine. As you do, you are trying to find a still spot to focus your attention – that point is your focus, and it is where all your breath travels to and where it comes back from. As you focus your breathing you start to allow the natural rhythm of your breathing to course through your body, and like a rudderless boat in open seas, you simply relax and allow yourself to ride each breath as it travels through your entire body, and back out. Focus only on your breathing. Even as you wander off to different thoughts, your breathing continues to bring you back like an anchor. Shamantha breathing has been shown to help deter age-based cognitive decline, and as such is one of the best breathing techniques to use while practicing meditation.

The next form of meditative breathing that is favored by practitioners is the Nadi Shondhana technique. This type of breathing is used as a purifying technique that originates from Hinduism. This meditative practice allows your body to find its inner balance by using controlled source breathing. Nadi Shondhana is known more widely as Alternate Nostril Breathing, where each side of the nostril is blocked while the other is used to breathe for a certain period of time to assist in the smooth flow of airflow. Each side is blocked for about thirty seconds to a minute each, and the body is taught to breathe through just one nostril at a time. The exercise generally lasts for about fifteen to twenty minutes, and doing so can help reduce high levels of blood pressure and help improve reactiveness. The breathing technique is particularly well known for allowing both hemispheres of the brain to get a physical and mental workout and can help with activities that require left and right motor senses to align.

Zhuanqi originates from Taoism and is a soft breathing technique that helps the body to harmonize with nature and their surroundings. The objective of Zhuanqi is simple. By uniting your breath in mind, you continue to breathe in and out, until your breathing has reached a gentle consistency. For beginners, the trick to understanding whether or not you are properly practising Zhuanqi is to notice when your breathing has gone absolutely quiet. Start by finding yourself a comfortable position, straighten your back and close your eyes, and as you do mentally focus your view on the tip of your nose. Carefully breathe in and out through your abdomen until you can hear your breathing start to quiet down. Your abdomen should be moving deeply outward with each breath that is drawn and inward as you expel the breath. As you do so, try to keep your diaphragm as still as possible, and repeat.

Khumbhaka Pranayamas, better known as the Antara and Bahya are two Hinduism inspired breathing techniques melded together to form what we refer to as intermittent breathing. The Khumbhaka Pranayamas are best practiced in an upright sitting position or alternatively in a standing posture. Prostate positions, or laying down are not advisable due to the nature of the exercise. To begin, expel all of the existing air in your lungs and then proceed to carefully inhale with your mouth until your lungs are once again full. In between breaths, once the air has been drawn in, hold the air in your lungs and after a brief pause begin to slowly release the breath. After emptying out your lungs, instead of automatically drawing in your next breath abstain for about 3 to 4 seconds. This is known as Bahya; this short deprivation will allow you to breathe in deeper and hold your breath longer, as the cycle repeats.

The Box Breathing technique uses a combination of slow breaths, and is predominantly practiced to relieve stress or anxiety. Unlike the other meditative breathing techniques mentioned here, Box Breathing, also commonly known as four-square breathing, can help regulate multiple pulmonary diseases including COPD or chronic obstructive pulmonary disease, and asthma. Similar to the Khumbhaka Pranayamas, you begin the process by expelling the excess air from your lungs and drawing in fresh air. However, as you draw in air, you breath to a slow count of four. You then hold your breath for four seconds, and then finally release the breath to the count of four before repeating the process.

Seating and Posture

We will start by discussing the five basic meditative postures. Your job is to identify which posture works for you in most situations and try to stick to it. While certain meditative practices do require you to follow a specific meditative posture, most of them can be adapted to alternative postures as well.

Chair Meditation

Because most of us tend to work 9-to-5 jobs, realistically speaking we do tend to spend most of our time seated in an office chair of some sort. Chair meditation is a great way to break your midday monotony without ever having to leave your station. For seated meditation, you're going to want to straighten your back and ensure that you are touching the floor with your feet. Ideally your knees should be bent at a 90-degree angle, and your back should be as straight as possible. If you're not sure what you want to do with your hands, try simply resting them on your knees.

Standing Meditation

Sometimes you want to get out of your chair, and may be more comfortable trying a standing method. You're going to want to start by standing so that your feet are at your shoulder length apart. Bend your knees slightly, and allow pressure of your entire day to ease out through your body all the way down to your feet. As you do so adjust your hands so they are placed gently across your stomach, so that you can feel every breath that moves through your body as you embark on your personal mission.

Cross-legged Meditation

Another posture you can explore if you feel comfortable, is the traditional Indian cross-legged sitting posture. This particular posture is actually the most commonly recommended posture from meditative activities, the idea is to keep your legs crossed under each other, with your hips elevated slightly higher than the heels of your feet. If you are new to meditation, it is generally recommended that you try this posture with a cushion or a towel or some sort of soft surface underneath you so that you don't hurt yourself, since it can be difficult to hold if you are not used to it. If you feel there's too much pressure on your heels, try bringing one of your legs across the other so that the ankle of one is positioned on top of the knee of the other leg. You could alternatively bring full heels across the thighs of the opposite leg in what is commonly known as the Lotus position.

The Burmese position is slightly different in that you don't cross your legs. Instead, you can position your feet so the ankles of each foot are bent inward and facing towards the pubic area – this posture is generally preferred by those individuals who find it difficult to cross their legs.

Kneeling Meditation

If you want to keep your spine straight but don't feel comfortable crossing your legs, another great alternative is to kneel. Traditionally, this is known as the Virasana or the Vajrasana. Here you start by bending your knees and resting your body weight along the length of your shins. Your ankles should be tucked under your bottom. For ease and comfort, you can opt to insert a rolled yoga mattress or a tube of some sort between your bottom and your knees.

This particular position is customarily easier than the cross-legged position, and is also generally pain-free, so your ankles will thank you.

Horizontal Meditation

If however none of these positions suit you, or you are trying a sleep inducing meditation, you will find that the posture of choice is generally the horizontal posture. As you lay down, be careful to ensure that your feet are parted at shoulder length, similar to the standing meditation posture, and your arms are laying at your sides instead of folded across your body. If you find this posture uncomfortable, you can bend your knees and elevate your hips slightly to help adjust yourself.

7. What is Hypnosis ?

Hypnosis is a procedure in which a guide, hypnotist or an operator gives suggestions to a subject during a state of focused awareness. If your attention is focused on any powerful suggestion, like "Visualize in your mind the most peaceful and relaxed place you ever could imagine. Imagine you are hearing your beloved grandmother's voice", the phenomenon of hypnosis tends to ensue. You start entering a light state of "trance". If you continue doing this over a longer period of time (say greater than 10 minutes), you tend to go to a much deeper level. You might have experienced listening to a very talented storyteller. He/she can make you go even deeper, especially if the story is interesting. At times, you seem to lose touch with reality and imagine yourself to be the hero of the story with tears dropping down your cheeks. You go even more deeply into this experience as you don't know what suggestions/visualizations, the storyteller would use next. Such is the power of hypnosis.

What is a trance state?

Frankly speaking, a relaxed, quiet, accepting and inwardly focused state is most useful for self-healing, stress management and change of undesirable habits. In self-hypnosis, this is the state of mind which is the usually aimed for. It allows deeper self-awareness as well as the ability to access the sub-conscious mind and thereby, change the physiological and behavioral patterns. Hence, trance is a very natural and simple state of mind, the state entered when your physical body goes to sleep while your mind stays awake. The frequency of your brain waves also changes in response to the changed level of your mental activity.

You can achieve this state by following a series of "suggestions". Suggestions are possible ways of thinking offered by a hypnotist to the subject. Hypnotist may ask you to visualize yourself to be in a calm and serene environment which may, though partly appear real. You could obviously choose not to hold that mental imagery in your mind as you and only you have the power to think what you want to see in your mind's eye. However, if you do allow yourself deliberately to follow the suggestions that the guide offers you, then you are much more likely to gain the benefits of a self-hypnosis program. So, in a very real sense, all hypnosis is actually self-hypnosis.

What is self-hypnosis?

Hypnotherapists refer the term "self-hypnosis" to the procedure in which a person is providing the suggestions to himself or herself in a calm and relaxed state of mind. Those who have been practising this activity are able to give suggestions to themselves without the use of any device or other person. They have attained a high level of control over various functions of their mind by practice alone which doesn't allow them to drift into sleep while hypnotising themselves. They can clearly induce themselves into trance state, provide the exact number of suggestions to their subconscious mind and wake up exactly on time as if their mind was on a software repair. However, as a beginner, you are recommended to make use of any audio recording device which would guide you through the procedure of self-hypnosis.

The real "payload" of the whole hypnotic process is carried by "Suggestions". The advantages of self-hypnosis over hypnosis by a guide are many. You can choose your own suggestions. You can literally "program" your mind with any motivation, any habit, any goal, any state of happiness or love you want just by simply recording the proper suggestions into the recording device and playing it while in a relaxed state of mind. You can do it at any time of the day however, doing it daily for a proper number of days, is what matters.

How Does the Self-Hypnosis Work?

How does your mental state influence you?

You might have noticed that your state of consciousness changes every day. It sometimes changes several times a day. In one moment you are feeling very enthusiastic, and in another, completely bored. You might feel very unresponsive for one moment, and in the next, very romantic. Sometimes you feel like doing heroic deeds in mind and sometimes you are caught by the cops while playing role of a villain or a bank robber in your mental imagery.

You can use self-hypnosis programs to help you change from one mood or state of mind, to another. Each mood is a type of mini-hypnotic state. Thus, there actually exists no specific state that can be termed truly "not hypnotic" – unless and until it is pure enlightenment!

Imagine you are on a holiday with your family to another country when you're feeling great, and then suddenly you get really bad news: your phone rings and you get informed that your house collapsed due to earthquake in your homeland. That news suddenly changes your mood and your thoughts. It also changes what you say and what actions you would take now.

Next, imagine that a couple of minutes later, you get another call from your friend informing you that the previous one was just a prank and the truth is that your lottery ticket has been selected and you have won the lottery worth a hundred thousand dollars. There would be, presumably, a dramatic change in how you feel. Ask a question to yourself, what got changed? Actually, nothing has physically happened to you, except that on both the occasions, the mental image of yourself and that of the world changed.

Likewise, if people in a receptive state of trance are told that they have just touched poison ivy, they can simply break out in a rash; if they are told there is a bag full of onions near them, they say they are actually smelling onions; if they are told that they are naked outside their home on a cold snowy day, they would begin to shiver. This happens because there is a direct connection between your body and the imagery that you hold in your mind – the self-hypnotic techniques help you use this connection for really improvising your life. You can use the techniques of self-hypnosis to heal more rapidly, improve your performance, manage stress, change your behavioural patterns, and above all, become the person you want to be.

How Hypnotherapy Works?

According to Sigmund Freud, the founder of Psychoanalysis, the human mind can be divided into three distinct realms of consciousness - the conscious, the subconscious and the unconscious. Each part can be thought of on a scale of depth.

Freud said that our conscious mind is the shallowest or top part of the mind. It is responsible for sensing all the things that we are directly aware of.

Freud believed that the subconscious mind is below the consciousness most of the time, situated a deeper level of mind. It is therefore difficult to (but not impossible to) access. It controls how we may react to or feel under certain circumstances or situations, based on what we already have learnt in the past through experience. It is also responsible for controlling and regulating the essential functions of our body, such as breathing.

The unconscious mind was regarded by Freud as the deepest part of our mind which is most difficult to reach. It contains the suppressed memories of any traumatic or highly emotionalized events.

By reaching a relaxed state, it is possible for us to sink deeper and deeper into our minds and thus reprogram or rewrite our subconscious. This is how hypnotism works. It is through the physical and mental relaxation that self-hypnosis allows people to bypass their conscious minds and thus, introduce desirable positive ideas and thoughts into their subconscious. When you 'awaken' from the state of self-hypnosis, the seeds of new ideas and thoughts in the subconscious will, eventually, begin to sprout out in the conscious mind and thus, can lead to changed behaviours. I would like to elaborate (and modify) a famous quote: "Constantly thinking positive makes you possess positive beliefs. Your positive beliefs make you generate more positive thoughts. Your thoughts make you utter positive words. Positive words plead you to take positive actions. Positive actions lead to a positive and successful destiny."

History of self-hypnosis

The phenomenon of hypnosis is known to man since time immemorial. The earliest evidence of practical usage of hypnosis by man is provided by the Tomb of Isis located in ancient Egypt wherein the Hieroglyphics show worshipers experiencing hypnotic sleep. In fact, the proper term used for this practice in ancient Egypt is "curing sleep." The ruler or a priest placed people in a specific mental condition and suggestions were used to treat illnesses.

Moving to ancient Greece, we find statues that depict trance like states. Historians and archaeologists say that these statues were created more than 2,000 years ago.

Other historical evidences claim that primitive societies made use of hypnotic phenomena throughout the ages for the sake of spiritual as well as physical benefits. Ritual dances and tribal drums have been a part of hypnotic phenomena in societies of South America and Africa. In middle ages, the Kings of Europe would touch commoners with extremely remarkable results. Ministers and priests would use a laying-on of hands that would cause mental changes in their church members.

Mesmer

Frederick Anton Mesmer had compiled a thesis titled The Influence of the Stars and Planets as Curative Powers, in the year 1773. This thesis claimed that the stars, moon and the planets affected humans through a phenomenon called animal magnetism. This term was used to refer to an invisible yet highly energetic fluid that runs through the bodies of every single human being.

Mesmer also said that if we place magnets around a diseased person, it will help improve the flow of specific healthy fluids, thus restoring the person health of the person back to normal. You should also note that the famous word "Mesmerisation" has its origins in the work of Mesmer on hypnosis and animal magnetism.

Mesmer practiced this magnetism not only in his native Austria but in parts of Western Europe. He is known to have treated many cases of hysteria by using magnets. According to his theory, the magnet is able to cure with its physical properties by interrupting the magnetic field of the sick person. If a sick person came to him for treatment, he would simply pass a magnet over his/her body and the person's health would get restored and he would get better again.

It is said that this animal magnetism theory came to Mesmer's mind from his personal observation of a Catholic Priest, Father Gassner, who used to heal people by using laying-on of his hands and making numerous passes all over the patient's body. After studying Father Gassner very carefully, Mesmer theorized that it was this magnetic fluid circulating in human bodies that was affecting all these changes and healing.

Four primary fluids were labelled as fluids of concern. These included phlegm, blood, yellow bile and black bile. The major factor for good health was considered "keeping these fluids in harmony". This animal magnetism theory was perfectly sound at that time and coincided with Benjamin Franklin's discovery of the phenomenon of electricity and also with the recent advances in the field of astronomy.

In 1778, Mesmer moved to Paris and invented backquets there, the extremely large iron pots that were capable of holding many of his patients. Mesmer would then line the backquets with magnets and iron filings. The subjects would enter this bath, immerse themselves into water and leave totally cured of their ailments. Mesmer became quite famous for his high percentage of cures.

In 1784, a commission to study Mesmer and his techniques was set up by the French Academy of Sciences. The internationally famous scientists were asked to investigate animal magnetism. These included Lavoisier, Benjamin Franklin and Dr. Guillotin, a chemist and inventor of the guillotine.

Mesmer used to take two large iron rods and touch them to several trees in the forest in order to magnetize them. His subjects were asked to touch these magnetized trees. It was a usual business for Mesmer since a lot of patients were cured of their afflictions. However, these afflicted people were not just touching the magnetized ones, but all the trees in the forest. These internationally acclaimed scientists arrived at the unanimous conclusion that Mesmer was not actually healing the patients. But the question arose that how come his patients were getting healed?

These patients were getting healed by using their own power. Mesmer stimulated patient's imagination in such a way that would enable him to be completely healed! This was not any black magic, but the magic of natural healing power of one's mind which is generated mostly under the phenomenon of hypnosis. This experiment clearly demonstrates that all hypnosis is actually self-hypnosis.

All of us have the power to create a positive change within us. All we need to do is to stay calm, relaxed and focussed on what we want to achieve, be it physical healing or personal development.

Elliotson

You might have heard about the inventor of stethoscope, Dr. John Elliotson. He was a professor of surgery at the University College in London, England. He was a big supporter of Mesmer and used "Mesmerism" on many of his patients to reduce the pain due to surgical incisions. He also used Mesmerization for the perfect cure of mental disorders.

Although, the other surgeons at this college condemned his practice by thinking that he was a quack, they still kept his stethoscope.

Braid

Dr. James Braid, the Scottish physician, lived from 1795-1860. Braid is sometimes referred to as the father of modern hypnosis. He is also known for actually coining the term, hypnosis. He presumably took it from Hypnos, a Greek word meaning sleep.

Later, Dr. Braid theorized that the hypnotic subject is never really in a state of sleep. So he changed this word to monoideism. Monoideism refers to "one thought" or "one word". Dr. Braid also felt that the hypnotic subject was so much focused on one idea or thought to the exclusion of all other thoughts that a trance like state ensued. Although, he put it right, and modern principles of hypnosis are based on that of monoideism, this term never caught on and we still prefer to use the term "Hypnosis" instead.

Today

Today, hypnosis finds a number of uses. Dentists and medical doctors are helping patients control pain by this technique when other methods fail or patients become unresponsive to treatments. Psychiatrists and Psychologists are using hypnosis for diagnosing and treating many kinds of mental illnesses.

There are professional hypnotherapists and hypnotists that help people overcome addictions and bad habits.

The growing use of self-hypnosis is to achieve your personal goals and fulfil your utmost desires which have a hindrance situated within you, like procrastination, lack of confidence and so on.

Scientific background of hypnotherapy

It has been proven lately that hypnotism has an impact on the brain which can be measured scientifically.

Doctors from Stanford University had scanned the brains of some volunteers who were told that they were looking at coloured objects. The fact was that the objects were actually black and white.

A scan of their head revealed that the areas of the brain, that used to register colour, had increased blood flow. This indicated that these volunteers genuinely 'saw' colors in their eyes of the mind.

There has been more research in this field where in one study, the volunteers were hypnotised with the visualizations of playing tennis, while in reality they were just lying inside the scanning machine. The areas of brain which would have been functional while actually playing tennis were showing increased blood flow in the brain scans. This clearly indicates that our brain cannot distinguish between what actually happens and what it imagines over a prolonged interval of time.

Well, it can be said with firm support of scientific evidence that this "inability of the brain to distinguish between a real experience and hypnotically imagined experience" has tremendous benefits for humans. It thus confirms that professional hypnotists are scientifically sound in claiming that hypnotism has a profound effect on the functioning of our mind, as well as our body.

So, hypnosis can be used for many kinds of physical symptoms and diseases which are mostly due to the psychological component of the mind. Let's take the example of pain control. You sometimes get a cut in your finger while cutting fruits or vegetables with a sharp knife. It hardly registers in your mind. It is only after you look at the blood oozing out of your finger that you start to experience pain. Thus, we can reprogram our mind to imagine that there was no cut, no blood and no pain in any part of your limb and that your limb is feeling superfine and relaxed. This is the information that would be delivered to your mind and you would start getting better under the effect of natural healing mechanisms which work best when you are relaxed in your mind.

It is a clear fact in scientific community that positive thinking rewires your brain and so do the positive suggestions during hypnosis. When you feed your mind with positive suggestions about achieving something or with visualizations of having something already achieved, structural changes take place in your brain. These structural changes begin to help you transmute the suggested/imagined experience into its physical equivalent. You see things and opportunities which you never had seen before. You begin to find that every situation of your life is in a constant process of helping you.

8. Self-Hypnosis Sessions

Tthere are numerous hypnotherapists in the world and there have been a lot of such professionals in the past. Many of new hypnotherapists have started using their own superb hypnotic techniques while most of them recommend the commonly used but effective techniques of self-hypnosis. Here I shall discuss the most commonly used techniques so that you can use the one most palatable to you.. This combination is easier to follow at the beginner level as well as it is equally effective (in some cases more effective than using individual techniques). The combination that I have used is that of:

- Progressive relaxation

- Visualizations

- Direct hypnotic suggestions

This is the best possible combination for achieving your goals and the changes that you want in life. Later on if you want to try other methods of self-hypnosis, you can replace the progressive relaxation with the other methods discussed below (which would bring you into the trance state). However, keep the visualizations and hypnotic suggestions as such and in the given sequence as they are the like the root and stem of the tree of self-hypnosis which you are going to plant in your mind's garden in order to grow juicy and desirable fruits out of them. The techniques are discussed below:

1. Eye Fixation

The main aim of this technique of self-hypnosis is to focus your mind. It also makes you simulate going to sleep and works well for hypnosis as well as self-hypnosis.

This technique begins with raising your eyes upward and fixing your attention on a spot on the ceiling of your room and then maintaining focus on that spot. Then you have to give suggestions to yourself (you can record them if you are the beginner) that the muscles in your eyelids are growing so tired that these are feeling heavier and heavier with every passing second. The next suggestions would provide you the information that your eyelids are so heavy that all you want to do is let your eyelids close. Just rolling the eyes slightly upwards and then closing the eyelids is a signal to your subconscious mind that it's high time now to go to the sleep. However, you actually don't fall asleep but move into a state of trance.

2. Double Bind

This technique occurs when you provide a suggestion to yourself that actually possesses two choices within it. One of the two suggestions is much stronger than the other. People most often are likely to respond to the stronger suggestion.

Here are a couple of examples of the double bind technique:

I know my cook didn't like to fry and cook the chicken or to clean my room in my college days (I didn't have a servant for cleaning but paid the cook to do it). If I asked him to clean my room, he'd try to find a way to get out of cleaning the mess of my room (filled with tonnes of written paper sheets). If I ask him to fry the chicken properly before cooking it, again, he'd try and find a way to get out of the frying process (I am getting late, will fry next time, and eat only cooked this time and blah blah). But, if instead, I offered him a choice, here's what used to happen. First, I ask would him, "Do you want to clean my room today or do you want to spend the whole time frying the chicken properly before cooking it?" He knew he had to make a choice. So, instead of focusing on some way to get out of doing whatever I've had asked him to do, he used to focus on which he'd rather do. Though he didn't like to do either one, he would prefer frying the chicken over doing my room. The double bind used to occur because he didn't want to do either, but he had to make a choice. And he would make the choice that is slightly more emotionally compelling choice for him. He used to have a much better attitude frying the chicken because he was able to get out of cleaning my room. Not only did I used to have a tasty fried and cooked chicken for dinner, but I would also have the privilege of cleaning my room myself as I and only I can keep the mess of papers in an organised fashion in my room (I hated when others clean/disperse the stuff in my room. Shhhh... Secret, don't tell my cook about it).

If you are an alcoholic, you are often conflicted about quitting drinking. There is a part of you that wants to continue drinking in heavy amounts because you enjoy drinking alcohol, yet there is a part of you that wants to quit because you know that is what is best for you health-wise in the long run. So, here is a double bind for you: "You can continue to drink in heavy amounts and poison your liver till you get liver failure and cancer and die a very ugly and painful death, or you can choose to be a non-alcoholic and live a healthy, happy and long life." Continue to present this suggestion of double bind type to an alcoholic (or to yourself if you are the one) during the hypnosis sessions. There's a very nice chance that the person will quit.

In fact you can use the double bind technique in almost any type of you daily problematic situations.

3. Eye Catalepsy

A bit of double bind is utilized in this technique. You have to shut your eyes so tight that you can't open them even if you want to. After you reinforce this suggestion several times in various ways, try to open your eyes even though these are shut so tight that opening them would be impossible. This causes your eyelids to quiver slightly (similar to the REM state). After this suggestion, give yourself another set of suggestions to relax even deeper. This is indeed a very effective technique used in self-hypnosis.

4. Staircase Technique

This technique is also quite famous in hypnosis scripts. This can be easily utilized in self-hypnosis procedures. One of the commonly used suggestions is to imagine oneself going down the stairs taking one step at a time. With each step downwards, you need to double your relaxation. The idea of going down into much deeper state of mind is represented by the metaphor "going down". This is an effective way of deepening your state of trance.

5. Metaphors

It is quite common to use metaphors in self-hypnosis scripts. You can use them in the form of phrases, complex words, or even stories.

You could remain calm and detached and relaxed and simply observe the thoughts that metaphors present to you and see them as they really are. Metaphors allow your mind to make the relevant associations you need to make in order to solve your specific problems.

Metaphors are effective methods that land you up into self-hypnosis as the subconscious mind works best with imagery and symbols. The visual metaphors and symbols help you to effectively get a suggestion or a message across to your subconscious mind which gives you a good chance to make the suitable change you are seeking to make.

6. Progressive Relaxation

This is the most common and one of the most effective techniques used in self-hypnosis. The purpose of progressive relaxation is to help your mind to focus and your body to relax. This technique was first developed by Dr. Edmund Jacobson in the first part of 20th century. He claimed that a muscle is relaxed effectively by first tensing it for a few seconds and after that, releasing it. It is this tensing and releasing different muscle groups throughout the body that produces a state of relaxation.

You need to relax the different areas of your body, with one area at a time, until your body feels completely relaxed. The attentiveness which is required by you helps you to focus your mind to the exclusion of everything else.

7. Conversational Hypnosis

Conversational hypnosis is said to have evolved out of the Ericksonian hypnosis, which is a branch of hypnosis named after Milton Erickson. This includes the use of double binds, indirect suggestion and confusion techniques. The formula for conversational hypnosis: rapport, confusion, and suggestion. And here's one such illustrated example.

When you are talking to yourself during hypnosis, and you already have a complaint/problem regarding enough workload at your office or overburden of studies at college, you need to first establish rapport and trust with the inner critic that lays insides you and holds you back. You can do this simply by agreeing with your inner critic. "That's so bad. Sounds like I have a lot of work to do there." Now, you have established rapport.

Now, you need to do a double bind by giving such a suggestion to your inner critic that has two choices within it. In this case, your inner critic will respond to the stronger part of your suggestion. "Even though I have a lot of work to do there, I never know when (small pause) I am going to feel better." This is the simplest form of a double bind. Now, your inner self is presented with two contrasting situations of feeling overloaded with work and feeling better. The phrase "I am going to feel better" is stronger because your inner self would certainly like to feel better. So your mind shifts from thinking about your feeling of being overloaded and exhausted with work to the likelihood of feeling better.

Then, in another minute, you have to offer a suggestion. "I am feeling better already." And that is what manifests.

When I got selected in my medical school, I found that my batch mates were feeling sad and depressed, right from the first month, about the long and tough journey of MBBS they had to go through than feeling happy about being selected in their favourite field of medicine. The factor of being away from their homes (Our medical school was located about 350 kilometres away from home city and there were almost no holidays to go back to home). I did not want to be influenced by those negative thoughts and depressive feelings, so I took help from self-hypnosis and used this technique of conversational hypnosis to tackle with the situation that I was in. I gave myself the following three suggestions:

1. I know that it is going to be a very hectic journey for 5 long years and I accept that it is very hard to study such huge medical books that took away from the compassion and comfort of my home (establishing rapport).

2. I can start getting sad about my upcoming hectic life for 5 years and come out of the med school as a depressed and negative person with negative results or I can choose to live life as a happy person who finds good in every situation, no matter how tough the situation is and come out of the medical school as a very happy, positive and successful person (Double bind).

3. I am already finding good in every situation and living a happy life (Suggestion).

That is what got manifested. All along my undergraduate medical career, I was being questioned frequently by my batch mates, seniors, juniors about the cause of my happy, positive and fun-loving nature in comparison to the frustrations, tensions and extreme stress that my batch mates used to go through around the days of exams. They also used to ask me how I used to get top scores in exams when I didn't resort to stress (being sad and under stress during exam days was wrongly perceived as having enough motivation for studies... What nonsense!). I chose to live positively through self-hypnosis and that was the secret of my positive results, never resorting to any addiction for counteracting stress (as I chose not to let stress overcome me) or never showing any signs of being sad or depressed.

8. Indirect Suggestions

This involves the use of metaphors and general suggestions that allow you to use your own mind in order to formulate an answer to the problem in hand. This technique can also be used to bypass your conscious or unconscious resistance for a direct suggestion. An example of the use of an indirect suggestion is given below:

Let's say you are back to home after a long tiring day, yet you are unable to take a short or long refreshing nap due to some issues and quarrelsome talks that happened during the day. After keeping yourself into a comfortable position, and taking a few deep breaths, give yourself the following indirect suggestions: "Aren't my eyelids feeling too heavy? Am I not tired of keeping my eyes open? Am I not tired of thinking too much throughout the day? Isn't it nice to let my eyes close? This is the time I should see a nice refreshing dream, Isn't it?" These indirect questions/commands force your subconscious mind to interpret them as "fall asleep now" and you will surely.

9. Guided Imagery

This is the technique which you can use to focus your mind on some journey and then to deepen your hypnotic state. Guided imagery journeys take you deep within your mind thereby deepening the hypnotic state. Often phrases along with metaphors and some embedded suggestions are utilized in your self-hypnosis script to make you go deeper. You can guide yourself on a journey deep into the mountains or woods. Guided imagery really helps to focus your mind.

10. Visualization

This is one of the commonly used as well as important techniques of self-hypnosis. In fact, visualization is a key component of any good self-hypnosis project. This is on account of a simple reason that our subconscious mind responds best to imagery and symbols. Frankly speaking, our subconscious mind does not recognize the words or sentences, but the hidden images behind them. You have to visualize what you desire in order to create its physical equivalent or change/modify some behaviour in your personality.

You simply need to visualize your success. In case you want to lose some weight, you have to visualize yourself as a trimmer, fit and slimmer version of yourself. You should keep this thing in mind that visualizing the end result is what is important. You don't have to visualize the hurdles that would come in the pathway between you and your goal. You have to see the end result as if it already has already been established. Just make sure to keep your visualization vivid and fixed in your mind as possible. Hold onto it not only during the self-hypnosis session, but also during any time of the day when anything reminds you of your goal. You are more likely to succeed if you consistently envision your success.

11. Post-Hypnotic Suggestions

The post-hypnotic suggestions are ones that you feed yourself during the self-hypnosis session in order to get yourself to act on those suggestions at a later time. Usually, a trigger is employed to activate the suggested behavior.

Let's take an example. If you want to stop your unusual habit of being a habitual smoker, give yourself a post-hypnotic suggestion that whenever you would carry a cigarette towards your lips and are just about to light it up, you would immediately become aware that you are about to burn your lungs, stain your teeth and discolour your lips. Suggest it to yourself that you would stop without any delay because of your powerful desire to have charming teeth and lips that would be noticed by everyone and compliment you on. The trigger used for this post-hypnotic suggestion is the movement of the cigarette from the packet towards your lips. It works like a charm because almost everyone has a powerful desire to have a charming and attractive teeth and lips that would be admired by everyone. I am sure that you would quit the smoking soon.

12. Direct Suggestions

Direct suggestions are the types of suggestions that you give to yourself in self-hypnosis to instruct or guide yourself to respond in a certain desired way. They have to be simple, to the point and literal.

You can guide yourself into a relaxed hypnotic state by using direct suggestions in the present continuous tense:

"I am taking a deep breath and allow myself to relax."

"I am relaxing my bodily muscles. I am relaxing all the muscles in my body. I am relaxing them deeply."

Direct suggestions can also used to change behavior:

"I am a truthful person."

"I am relaxed and calm in all situations."

13. Confusion Technique

It is a rarely used hypnosis technique. If you seem to have difficulty with the normal induction technique for reaching a hypnotic state, then you should use confusion technique.

Let us try to understand this technique with the help of an example. If you are a woman who respects the opinion of her husband, and his words usually do make sense when he is talking, then you'll pay attention to him. Occasionally, when he seems to be saying something much important to you, but you can't understand the meaning clearly, you will assume that you need to pay more attention in order to grasp what he is saying. Now, suppose a point is not logically clear, in hope of understanding what he is saying, you will focus more and more of your attention. And you already know that focusing your attention is the key component of hypnosis (or self-hypnosis).

9. Deep Sleep Hypnosis Sessions

Welcome.

This is going to be a thirty-minute guided hypnosis session to help you drift off into a deep and relaxing sleep. The most important thing to do while listening to this session is to keep an open mind. You must go with the flow, listen to my voice, and remember to breathe.

Remember, it is not always possible to enter a light hypnotic state on the first try, but we are going to try as I guide you gently and smoothly into this state so you can fall asleep. Please bear in mind that you are not going to enter any sort of deep catatonic state. Nothing is going to be physically altered within the realm of your mind. The process of hypnosis and this guided meditation is extremely safe, and you are in control of it.

Now, I want you to get comfortable. Because you are trying to achieve a deep sleep, you should be lying down, your head resting on your most comfortable pillow and you are warmed by your softest blanket. Lie back and let your shoulders go slack, relaxing against the cushion of your bed. Gently close your eyes and release all the tension from your muscles. Release the tension in your arms, then your legs. Let go of the tension in your chest and in your back. All of the muscles in your body begin to feel looser and looser and your body is feeling light.

Next, tighten the muscles in your calves and hold for one, two, three seconds. Now release the muscles. Tighten them again for one, two, three seconds. Now release. The excess energy that keeps you up at night has been expelled from your calves. Your calves are now ready for sleep.

Next, squeeze your thigh muscles and hold for one, two, three seconds. Now release. The tension that was once stored there has been released. Your thighs are now ready for sleep. Feel the lightness that has cloaked your legs. Your legs feel weightless as if they could float up to the ceiling.

Focus your attention on your buttocks. Tighten your muscles in buttocks for one, two, three seconds. Now release the muscles. The tightness in your buttocks and lower back has been relieved. Your buttocks and lower back are now ready for sleep.

Focus your attention on your abdomen. Squeeze your abdominal muscles for one, two, three seconds. Now release. The anxiety that has been stored up and deterring sleep has been released. Your abdomen is now ready for sleep.

Concentrate on your chest. Tighten the muscles in your chest for one, two, three seconds. Now release. The sadness that has been weighing on you and preventing your mind from resting has been expelled. Your chest is now ready for sleep.

Direct your attention now to your shoulders. Tighten the muscles in your shoulder for one, two, three seconds. Now release. The stress that has been building in the deep tissue of your shoulders has now been dissolved. Your shoulders are now ready for sleep.

Focus your attention on your neck. Gently tighten the muscles and hold for one, two, three seconds. Now release. Gently tighten the muscles in your jaw and hold for one, two, three seconds. Now release. Gently tighten the muscles in your mouth and hold for one, two, three seconds. Now release. Gently squeeze your eyelids tighter for one, two, three seconds. Now release. The tension that was held in your face has now been released.

The entirety of your body has been washed with serenity as you expel the negative energy from your muscles. Now that your body is relaxed, your mind can now relax in preparation for deep slumber. Realize how free it feels to let go of all built up tension. In this moment nothing else matters. You are free. You are relaxed. You are weightless.

There is nowhere for you to be and you have everything you need. You are here, in this moment, permitting the calming sensation to course through your body. Your thoughts drift away. You don't try to follow or catch them. With each breath you take, you are feeling more and more serene. Breathe in, welcoming peace and harmony to your soul. Breathe out, exhaling all the negative energy and releasing your control. Realize how good it feels to be so relaxed.

Focus on being as relaxed as you can be at this moment. Allow your mind to settle down a little, to quiet, to be still. Instead, focus more on your body. How does it feel lying in your bed? Examine the coziness you feel beneath your sheets. Feel how smooth your sheets are and gentle weight of your blanket on top of you. Relax in the embrace of the softest bed in the world. You are content in every way.

Imagine that on the other side of the room is an open fire crackling. The orange and yellow flames emanate a sensation of calmness as its soft light can be seen upon your walls and ceiling. You feel the warmth of this sensation. You watch closely as the flames flicker and dance upon the logs. The sound of the crackling fire reminds you that you are safe in this space. In this bed you are warm, cozy, and protected.

Scan your body for tension. Find where you still hold stress in your body. Examine your shoulders, your neck, your temples, and your back. Find the stress that is hiding and release it. Allow your body to feel relieved, relaxed, at peace.

Examine the aroma of the fire as it fills the room. The fragrance is deep and musky. It reminds you of good memories with the ones who love you. These memories remind you that your life is beautiful. Place both hands on your stomach, one below your ribs and one above your belly button. Take a deep breath in through your nose, inhale those good memories. Let the air fill your belly and your hands rise on top of your abdomen. Then, through your nose, exhale all of the negativity you have collected. The worries that you harbor are no longer welcome here.

Breathe in the relaxing scent of the fireplace, fill up your stomach like it is a balloon. Let your hands move as your inhale. Then exhale any remaining tension. You now feel loose and at ease. There is a calmness that envelopes your body as you breathe. As you feel more relaxed, you hear only the fire in this quiet space. The quietness of the room also quiets your mind and you welcome rest and relaxation.

As you lay, keep breathing and reveling in this blissful setting: you're tucked inside your cozy bed with a fire to keep you warm. Focus on this serene moment and give yourself permission to enjoy it. Remember that you are in control. Many times, your mind is overthinking, overanalyzing, and too critical. In this moment, it is you who is in control and you will exhale those negative thoughts. As you exhale, you regain your balance and you feel content. Your body feels looser, lighter, and a weight is lifted off your chest.

Your body is light and warm as you listen to my voice. Let me guide you as you drift off. I'm going to count now and you will listen. Let my voice lull you. You are safe and relaxed and warm.

Ten… Your body is entirely loose and relaxed.

Nine… You are in a peaceful, calm, and safe environment.

Eight… You can feel the warmth and love of those who care about you, enveloping your senses.

Seven… The sound of the burning fire, the crackling of wood lulls you further into an even deeper state of relaxation.

Six… You inhale all of the good in the world with each breath you take.

Five… You exhale all the bad, expelling all of your stress and anxiety with each breath out.

Four… You feel your body getting lighter until you are almost like a feather in the breeze.

Three… You feel your mind becoming heavier and brimming with warmth and love.

Two… Accept the peace that has engulfed you, understand that it is good. Let it send you off ever deeper into the feeling of relaxation.

One… You feel yourself drifting all the way down, as deep as you can go, nearer to the bottom, towards warmth and sleep.

You are safe and you are relaxed. Allow yourself to feel safe and relaxed in this space.

Imagine that you are a leaf on a tree. You are connected to a giant colony of other leaves attached to a branch. That branch is attached to a trunk. You are a part of a busy, ever rustling tree. However, you want to be still. You need to rest. You need to separate yourself from the busyness of your world. You decide that you will depart your branch and you begin to float. Slowly, as if gravity has slowed your fall, you twirl and roll in the breeze. You are peacefully drifting further and further, reassured that you are safe.

Instead of the ground, you see that there is a quiet pond below your tree and soon you will touch the surface. As you float towards it, you notice its stillness. There are no ripples or disturbances. The surface is smooth and clear; it is as reflective as a mirror. As you reach the water, you greet the surface with a delicate kiss.

You send gentle, peaceful ripples from your contact. Concentric circles echo out to the edges of the pond. This energy radiates from you until the last ripple falls away. It is now you on the water, undisturbed and immersed in the tranquility of your setting. You drift on the surface of your unconsciousness. You feel the warmth of the water beneath you and surrounding you. The water is so soothing that you feel yourself getting heavier. You feel as though you could keep floating deeper and deeper beneath the surface until you fell asleep.

The relaxation that you feel now is beckoning you closer to rest, to deep sleep. Notice how relaxed you are in this very moment. Notice how soothing the sensations are in your body. Breathe in the relaxation that the water provides. Breathe out any tension you have.

I am going to count down from five. When I reach one, you are going to fully embrace the peace that has engulfed you and lose yourself in sleep. You will feel yourself slipping into a calm and serene rest.

Five… You think of the still surface of the pond, and how it provided safety for you, the leaf. The calm water is summoning your sleep.

Four… You feel the warmth of tranquility ripple from the top of your scalp and down your neck. It glides through your shoulders, radiates through your chest and stomach, and finally glazes over your legs. You are encompassed by this sensation.

Three… You feel your body become heavy and you softly sink in a little deeper to your consciousness. You are safe and protected.

Two… You feel yourself drift away, like your leaf on the still pond. You float away, quietly into the night.

One… You are now asleep, resting and at peace.

Breathe in, Breathe out. Breathe in, Breathe out. When you wake up, you will be renewed and refreshed and ready to take on the day. You will be ready to conquer the obstacles of your life now that you have conquered sleep.

Deep Sleep Hypnosis Session 2

Welcome.

This is going to be a thirty-minute guided hypnosis session to help you drift off into a deep and relaxing sleep. The most important thing to do while listening to this session is to keep an open mind. You must go with the flow, listen to my voice, and remember to breathe. Remember, it is not always possible to enter a light hypnotic state on the first try, but we are going to try as I guide you gently and smoothly into this state so you can fall asleep. Please bear in mind that you are not going to enter any sort of deep catatonic state. Nothing is going to be physically altered within the realm of your mind. The process of hypnosis and this guided meditation is extremely safe, and you are in control of it.

Now, I want you to get comfortable. Because you are trying to achieve a deep sleep, you should be lying down, your head resting on your most comfortable pillow and you are warmed by your softest blanket. Lie back and let your shoulders go slack, relaxing against the cushion of your bed. Gently close your eyes and release all the tension from your muscles. Release the tension in your arms, then your legs. Let go of the tension in your chest and in your back. All of the muscles in your body begin to feel looser and looser and your body is feeling light.

Listen to the sound of my voice. Let it wash over you and soothe you. Release all your stress. Release every anxiety and open your mind. Allow yourself, in body and mind, to be gently carried away. Allow yourself to be lulled into a sense of calming security. You are safe. Sway your head back and forth in the smallest of motions, just enough for you to feel the heaviness of your skull. Move it back and forth, slower and slower until you feel that you are starting to get more relaxed. When you feel the relaxation wash over you, you can slowly stop. Rest your head and feel your skull settle into the back of your head.

Take a large breath in, hold it in your belly for one, two, three beats and then let it out. Breathe in deeply through your nose and breathe out through your mouth. Continue to breathe deeply as you slowly move your focus to your toes, warm and snuggled in your blanket. Gently curl your toes as you feel the warm sensation of peace move from the very tips of your toes upwards. The warm sensation fills your foot and slowly rolls towards your ankles and finally tingles up your calves. All the tension in your muscles floats away as the warmth moves upwards once more. It moves past your calves and swims towards the curves of your knees. It continues to travel higher and higher. Notice how your legs are feeling heavy and you are feeling calmer than before. There are no worries anymore, only this heavy warmth. Give in to the sensation that fills your body from the toes upwards. Drift into a deeper feeling of serenity and tranquility with every breath that you take.

Breathe in. Now breathe out. Slowly, gently, deeply. Breathe in. Breathe out. That peaceful warmth of relaxation continues to spread. It moves past your waist and into your stomach. It meanders over each of your ribs, wandering towards your chest. This warm feeling calms you, soothes you. All your worries begin to fade away into dust, taken away with the breeze, and you let them go, the same way you let go of your shoulders and your back as your muscles loosen even more and you feel light like air.

Your arms are beginning to feel light too. The warmth spreads to your shoulders, and travels to your elbows and now your wrists, your hands and now your fingers. Let them feel warm and light. Let go of the desire to resist the peaceful sensation that washes over you. Release the control over your body and give into this calming sensation. Relax your neck, loosen your jaw. Release the tension in your face and in your forehead.

Realize how free it feels to let go of all that tension. In this moment nothing else matters. You are free. You are warm. You are light. There is nowhere for you to be. You have everything you need. You are here, in this moment, allowing the relaxing sensation to flow through your body. Your thoughts drift away, but some stay. You let them. You don't try to follow or catch them. You must let them be. You let them simply float through and pass on their way out. With each breath you take, you are feeling more and more serene. Breathe in, welcoming peace and harmony to your soul. Breathe out, exhaling all the negative energy and releasing your control. Realize how good it feels to be so relaxed.

Your body is light and warm as you listen to my voice. Let me guide you as you drift. I'm going to count now and you will listen. Let my voice lull you. You are safe and relaxed and warm.

Five… You think of the word from the carving in the tree bark. Your special word. It melts away every remaining tension until your body and mind are relaxed. It is summoning your sleep.

Four… You feel the warmth of peace move from the top of your head and down your neck. It moves through your shoulders, radiates through your chest and stomach, and finally glazes over your legs.

Three… You feel your body become heavy and you softly sink in a little deeper to your consciousness. You are safe and protected.

Two… You feel yourself drift away, like a leaf on a still pond. You float away, quietly into the night.

One… You are now asleep, resting and at peace.

Breathe in, Breathe out. Breathe in, Breathe out. When you wake up, you will be refreshed and ready to take on the day. You will be ready to conquer the stresses of your life now that you have conquered sleep.

10.Hypnosis for Overthinking

N ow I would love to guide you on an amazing trip and remove your habit of overthinking everything. Let me start by bringing your focus to my voice. Pay attention to the strong force drawing you to my voice as I speak. This force grows stronger with every word I say.

Find yourself a comfortable and quiet space to sit or lay down, either is good. Make sure you are undisturbed and open the windows to feel the fresh air. Bring your focus back to my voice and pay close attention to the sounds around you. The sound of relaxing music and my voice are the only two sounds you can hear now. I would love to use a method I once used on a friend for this session. My friend was filled with fear that stopped her from doing what she wanted. It caused her to overthink every possible task before jumping in.

Enough about that now. I want you to focus on your breathing as you lay or sit as comfortably as possible. Take a deep breath in and hold it for a moment. Now release it slowly. Pay attention to the air as it crosses your lips and take note of how it feels. Can you feel the tension crossing your lips? Now I want you to think hard about a fear you have, a fear you face every day. One that has stopped you from doing something incredible. Now for the scary part. I want you to take a deep breath, sucking in the air around you. Hold it for a moment. Just a little longer. Now force that air out. The air you inhaled was polluted by your fear. You have taken the first step to facing your fear.

Keep your thoughts with my voice as I help you relax your tense muscles now. Carry on taking deep but gentle breaths now and hold each one for just a moment. Exhale softly, without too much force this time. Don't stop doing this. I want you to listen inside. Can you hear it? Can you hear the racing beat of your heart? Allow the rapid beat of your heart to be second to the sound of my voice.

I want you to start with your head. Tense your head by allowing anger to possess it. Hold this tension for a few seconds. One, two, and release slowly. Take note of the way your head feels now. The fear that was stored in your muscles has been crushed by your tension. Next I want you to do the same with your neck and shoulders. Force your muscles into a tense position. Hold. One, two, and release. Notice how fearless they feel now.

Keep listening to my voice as I speak to you. Every word bringing you one step closer to relief. Move your focus to your arms and tense your muscles. Hold. One, two, and release. Listen to your racing heartbeat as your arms melt like jelly. You will repeat this exercise with your legs and feet next. Pull your legs into a straight and tense position and hold them like that. One, two, and release. Pay close attention to the absence of fear in your legs. A wonderful sense of relaxation overcomes them. Shift your attention to your chest area while you allow my voice to keep you calm. Feel your chest rise and fall with every breath you take, remembering to hold each breath for just a moment.

Listen to the rhythm of your heart. It's still racing but has slowed quite a bit now. Count every heartbeat until you get to ten. I will give you a moment to do this. Keep your breathing consistent throughout your counts. You can feel a calm effect traveling through your physical body. Your body is just melting into your bed or chair. I want you to breathe deeply and hold it. One, two, and release gently. Move your focus back to your heartbeat and count the beats again. One, two, three, four, five, six, seven, eight, nine, and ten.

I want you to bring your core focus back to my suggestion now and listen to every word. Feel safer with every word you hear. Allow your heartbeat to move back to a secondary sound. It's important to keep it in earshot throughout the session. Now I want you to bring your imagination into full focus. Allow my voice to carry your imagination into an alternate place. You trust me and every inch of you believes that you can follow me.

Start opening your mind's eye slowly, allowing your imagination to take over. An image is developing in front of your mind's eye as it opens. You look down and notice that you are wearing odd clothes, not your own clothes. You are wearing a red jumpsuit with bright yellow stripes down the side. You want to touch it with your hand but you are wearing gloves. You can feel the cold leather around your skin. You start feeling weight on your back that wasn't there before, a heavy weight. Your head also feels heavier because you appear to be wearing a helmet. You notice someone sitting across from you as your image comes into focus. You know this person because she is a close friend. You can't hear her but you see her mouth moving. She must be talking. She is all dressed in the same ridiculous get up as you. You can feel the roar of an engine beneath you. The roar is trying to penetrate your mind but I am still here. Your guide is with you all the way.

There is a sudden gush of air that is deafening. You look to your right and there is a door that has been opened. The entire image is becoming clear now. You are on a small plane and have been suited up for a dive. Deep down inside you feel a small sense of calm despite your location. My voice has become deeper and louder now, penetrating your subconscious mind and soothing your fears. You shift focus to your heartbeat as you breathe and hold. One, two and release. Keep your breathing calm at all times. Your heartbeat is faster than normal but not too fast.

Suddenly, your subconscious mind wanders off to think about all the possible outcomes; trying to analyze all the risks of what you're about to do. Stop! Breathe deep and hold. One, two, and release the air and the fear along with it. You move closer to courage with every word I speak and every breath you take. You look down at your hands and see the tremors calm down, little by little. You listen to your heartbeat as you glance across at your best friend and she smiles at you. It's a genuine smile that slows your heart down more. Thump thump thump. You feel relaxed enough to return the smile.

You can feel your fears leaving your body as your smile stretches across your face. Your friend is speaking to you but the noises are cancelling her voice out. You focus hard on the sound of my voice and the peaceful music in the background. This takes your focus away from all the terrible noise and now you can start hearing your friend. She gets up and approaches you, telling you how proud she is that you have come with her. You want to utter negativity as she takes your hand but you control your urge and allow her to take your hand. You feel proud of yourself in this moment and you give her hand a reassuring squeeze.

Your friend asks if you're ready and you just nod in agreement as she gently pulls you up, never letting go of your hand. You feel relaxed with her touch and the sound of my voice guiding you. All terrible thoughts have stopped racing through your mind. You have chosen one and that is the thought of enjoying the dive from a small plane in the middle of nowhere. Nothing will go wrong now. You follow your friend closer to the door and she asks if you would like to keep holding hands. You nod in agreement again with a bigger smile this time.

Take a moment to listen to your heartbeat and the sound of my suggestions. Please be aware that your heart has stopped racing, it has slowed to a normal rhythm now. Take a deep breath in again and hold it there for a moment. You feel good as you release it. You take a step forward while holding your friends hand and look out the door. You can see the amazing fields below with the ocean just a short distance to the right. The gusts of wind no longer bother you. You cannot hear it anymore. You feel yourself take the final step forward while holding your friend's hand. You can feel her support in her touch.

You have the greatest sense of freedom as the two of you enter the freefall. You cannot describe the rush of positive emotions flowing through you. You feel your friend's hand in yours and relax into a euphoric state. You can feel your friend is in the same place. You are sharing an incredible experience with her. An experience you would surely have missed if you allowed your fear to control your thoughts. My voice momentarily becomes secondary to the joy you feel. You are falling and the fresh air is rushing past your skin. You can feel the droplets from the sea around your face. The sound becoming a faint whistle past your ears. Now I need you to come back to my voice and focus.

You use your free hand to pull the tag, releasing your parachute. There is a sudden tug when your parachute opens. Your friend lets go of your hand and you watch her move away to open her own parachute. She never removes her calming smile from her face for a single moment. This is the exact moment you realize you have conquered your fear and you have stopped thinking about all the things that could have gone wrong. You have finally allowed yourself to be free and you know you can't control everything.

You pay close attention to my suggestions as you approach your landing field. Continue breathing as you count backwards from ten. Ten, nine, eight, seven, six, five, four, three, two, and one. You feel your feet gently touch the ground as you are whisked away from your imaginary image and back to your bed or chair. You can feel the comfort and safety of your physical presence again. I want you to be aware of the smile you have naturally stretched on your face, a genuinely happy smile.

Take a deep breath. Hold it for a moment and release it gently. Listen to your heartbeat's perfect slow rhythm as you descend back into your own body. Take your right hand and place it on your chest and inhale. Hold it for a moment before you exhale slowly. Notice the rise and fall of your chest as your breath shows no sign of fear anymore. You feel more than free; you feel happy. No thoughts can take away an experience like this. Feel your body become heavier as you are relaxed into your bed or seat; your physical presence fully restored. Now breathe, open your eyes and feel like a new person.

11. Hypnosis for Procrastination

Welcome back to another session. We are going to focus on procrastination this time. Give in to my voice and allow me to carry you to a mindful space. Lie down and relax. Or sit down if you feel more comfortable doing so but this exercise is best when you are laying down. Make sure that you are in a room with a closed door and open windows. Feel the fresh breeze touch your skin softly as you sit there. Take a moment to think about why you are doing this. Focus on a single thought to make yourself aware of your reason for entering this state of mind. Close your eyes once you have it.

Visualize your idea in your mind, give it a shape and size. I will give you a moment to do this. Become aware of your surroundings while you're doing this. Start by focusing on the fibers of your duvet. Is it soft? Feel the duvet on your skin and listen to my voice as you take a deep breath and hold it for a second. Now release your breath slowly through your mouth.

Listen to the sound of the breeze. I know you can feel it but now I want you to listen to it. Listen to the faint whistle it makes as it passes through the window. Be aware of the fact that it's making a sound. Now I want you to rewind for a moment, back to your worrisome idea. The idea you have chosen to bring to the surface, something you have chosen to avoid for some time now. You are going to avoid it a little longer. Follow my instructions closely as you take your idea that now has a shape and wrap it in a fancy box. Close the box and feel your left hand place the imaginary box beside you. Remember that you have visualized an idea, a thought. It doesn't actually have a physical form.

Now I want you to focus deeper on my voice. Yes, you can do it. Return your left hand to your side and caress your duvet. Feel the intricate fibers between your fingers. Continue doing this while you inhale deeply and hold. One, two, and release. Remember to release your breath slowly because there is no rush. Now I want you to take your right hand and place it on your stomach and run your fingertips gently up and down your skin. Become aware of the connection between your fingertips and the skin on your stomach. You feel a light friction.

Open your mind to my suggestion and change your finger strokes from up and down, to circles. Focus on the friction between your fingers and skin. This sensation is what release feels like. The friction is your body's tension being drawn out by your fingertip movement. The friction is moving into your right hand and going up your arm. It travels through your chest area and into your left arm from there. Follow the friction as it travels down your left arm and into the duvet fibers you are holding with your fingertips. Keep inhaling gently, holding it each time for a moment before release. All your tension is leaving your body. Focus your awareness on the tension exiting through every breath you take, through every stroke of your fingers running over your skin.

You are listening to my voice on an even deeper level now. You can hear it inside your mind, telling you what to do. I want you to start moving your right hand and keep your left hand beside your body, holding the duvet. Don't disconnect yourself from this outlet. You will remove the outflow of your tension. Don't stop breathing gently while you move your right hand up and down your body to every place you can reach. Keep circling your fingertips and following the tension out of your left arm.

Now I need you to concentrate. I want you to start wiggling your toes gently. Focus on the movement and the way you feel as you do this. This helps to send the tension up to your circling fingertips. You won't miss any tension this way. Move your awareness to your level of relaxation once you feel comfortable. Your entire body has sunk into a relaxed state as my voice stays with you every moment of the journey. Every word I utter brings you one step closer to your comfort. You feel safe in the guidance you are allowing.

Now I want you to become aware of your new surroundings. It's time to awaken your mind's eye. You need to continue breathing deep and consistent breaths, pausing for a moment between each inhale and exhale. Shift your attention to your left hand beside you. Can you feel the leaves under your fingertips? Move your left hand around and become aware of the leaves around you. Now take your right hand and do the same. Listen to my voice as I help you feel your body on the pile of soft leaves. My voice is even deeper in your mind now. Controlling your hands through gentle guidance. You feel so calm and safe.

I want you to start creating an image. Pay close attention to my calm and instructive voice as my words become your image. Use your imagination to create this picture while you lay there and breathe consistently. I want you to count to ten. Count quietly in your mind. Now open your beautiful inner eyes and see what you have created. You are looking at tall trees standing over you with rays of sunlight dancing between them. You can feel yourself growing an urge to explore this beautiful nature before you as you raise yourself to a seated position. You see the prettiest purple flowers under the trees. They are bountiful with the perfect balance of sun and shade from the trees. Feel yourself rise as you approach the flowers to smell them.

My voice keeps guiding you as you walk toward the flowers and kneel down to pick one. You notice a small stairway leading downward behind the trees as you lift the fragrant flower to your nose and you feel a strong desire to follow the overgrown stairway. It looks like no one has been down here in awhile. Follow me down as I descend the staircase. You can see the stairway leads down to a wooden cabin as your foot touches the first step. The vegetation surrounding the cabin is beautiful and exotic, something from an unknown world. You feel the need to know more even though the cabin looks abandoned. You can smell all the amazing flowers as you descend step by step. Each step makes you relax a little more, each makes you feel safer.

You are enjoying the journey so much that you are falling behind. You will find my voice at the bottom of the stairway. You continue your descent, step by step. My voice gets louder as you catch up but you are also aware of the sounds around you. There are birds chirping in the trees and you are sure you can hear something in the bush. You still feel calm and safe because nothing can harm you here. You can hear water flowing over rocks in the distance. The flow of water is strong and seems to match your urge to get to the cabin. Take a moment to enjoy the sound. You don't need to rush to the cabin. It will come in good time.

You focus your attention back to my voice after a moment of reflection in this amazingly wild and untouched area. My voice is urging you to climb the three steps to the cabin door. You count the steps as you climb them. One, two, and three. The cabin looks more deserted now that you are closer. This doesn't persuade you to leave because you need to know what's inside. Before you do, take a deep breath in through your nose and hold. One, two, and slowly release the air from your mouth.

Let my voice guide you inside and focus on my every word. You feel more relaxed with each one. You place your hand on the door knob and feel the cold touch your skin. You feel yourself hesitate for a moment. Take a deep breath and hold. Release your hesitation through your breath. Now you are free to turn the knob. You push the door gently as you turn it. It creaks ever so slightly as you open it. You see piles and piles of boxes from floor to ceiling inside. Please don't be afraid and step inside.

You can feel the air is thicker here than outside. The cabin has been abandoned for too long now and is filled with dust bunnies. You proceed forward with my guidance anyway. You know where you are; you know exactly who abandoned this place. This is your subconscious cabin and it's overflowing with things that need to be taken care of. You feel the urge to tackle the tasks in the boxes as you stand there. Now listen to me carefully because I am aware that you feel confident now. I am also aware that you realize your problem but you need to become aware that you can't do it all at once.

Feel yourself accepting the fact and start organizing your boxes. You can separate them into four different corners. Inhale deeply through your nose and hold. One, two, and three. Now exhale gently as you see how the boxes have piled up. You are more than capable of working through them in an orderly fashion. Make one corner an urgent corner, the other corner can be for tasks which are less urgent, the third corner is for tasks that can wait a little and the last corner can be for tasks you must decide if you wish to proceed. Can you see how organized it all looks now? See how much easier it will be to finish these tasks? Now it's time to go home.

Listen to my voice to guide you back as you remain aware of your feelings and the sounds around you. Leave the door unlocked when you go. This is your safe house and no one will find it. Retrace your steps back up the staircase and pay attention to the vegetation around it. It's been cut back. It remains absolutely stunning but the stairway is clear. Take one more sniff of the flowers under the trees before you lay down on the leaves. Now I want you to focus on your breathing. Deep breath in and hold. One, two, and release gently. Lay your arms beside you and feel your surroundings. Become aware of the duvet under your fingertips. Breathe in deep and hold. One, two, and release the air gently. Feel your body return to its physical form. The cool touch of the breeze passing over you as the sound of the breeze passes through the window. Now I want you to reach to your left and pick up the box you placed beside you. Open it and visualize the one idea you stored in the box. This will be your first task to complete.

Focus on my voice as you feel your physical presence resuming itself. Now open your eyes and repeat after me. I am aware of my new strength and ability. Say it another three times. Notice how refreshed you feel, physically, and emotionally. Feel your burning desire to finish your task so you may visit your cabin again to collect another. My voice seems further and further away as you are now awake and fully aware of your present surroundings (Sealey, n.d).

12. How to Calm Emotions

Regardless of whether it's eating an additional slice of cake, or choosing to go after another job, your emotions influence all that you do. If you are to make every moment count and approach your everyday tasks in a positive manner, you should take care of your emotional health.

Having great emotional health implies you can deal with our emotions, thoughts, and feelings. You can settle on better choices and explore life's difficulties with certainty and versatility. Building your emotional health empowers you to feel content with yourself. You will appreciate important individual connections, and push ahead in life with a sense of purpose and direction.

The impact of emotions on the body

Regardless of whether it's with sweat-soaked palms or an outburst of laughter, your emotions are regularly accompanied by a physical reaction. You have probably experienced a flood of queasiness before accomplishing something nerve-wracking, or a shock of excitement at the possibility of an upcoming occasion.

However, the quick flashes of emotions that you feel in your body are just a little piece of the physical impact of emotions. Your body reacts to your emotional wellbeing from various perspectives — if you are feeling stressed or troubled, you may encounter physical indications, such as insomnia or sleep deprivation, or even hypertension and stomach ulcers.

Poor emotional wellbeing can also affect on your immune system, which is the reason you appear to get more coughs and colds when you are going through a really stressful season or when you are gripped by anxiety, or why you take more time to shake off illnesses when things are strenuous at work.

Also, obviously, when you are feeling somewhat down, you are more averse to taking an interest in the things that advance physical prosperity. When you feel down and out emotionally, or pressured, you are more likely to be tempted to grab an extra glass of wine or to eat unhealthily. Thusly, your emotions influence your basic decision-making skills at the time, which can have an impact on our physical wellbeing.

These physical sicknesses can be a useful sign to you that something isn't exactly great with your emotional health, so you can consider making a move to improve it.

The physical advantages of positive emotions

It's not all awful news. However — there are long haul physical advantages related to emotional prosperity as well, and perhaps the greatest benefit of positive emotional health is the positive effect it can have on your physical health.

For instance, you can likely envision how becoming hopelessly in love prompts feelings of bliss, calmness, and satisfaction; however, did you realize that it's also thought to support the development of new synapses, which improves your memory?

Specific Ways of Emotions Influence Your Health

Your emotions have an immediate connection with your body that gives them a chance to have a major effect on your psychological as well as on your physical state. With the correct learning, it's conceivable to perceive how ground-breaking your feelings are and how they can assist you with managing your perspective and keeping your body and mind sound.

Have you at any point thought about what you can do to your perspective on life and to the condition of your body with the assistance of the emotions that numerous individuals attempt to stow away? If you consider your emotions when they trouble you, you can help yourself as well as introduce harmony and calmness to your mind.

1. Love

When in love, you may experience a racing heartbeat and your hands getting sweatier. It is brought about by the incitement of adrenaline and norepinephrine, Simultaneously, oxytocin, the "love hormone," makes you feel glad, stable, and minimizes your pain as the "painkiller" zones of the mind are being actuated, and your heart ends up healthier. It is said that wedded individuals live longer than singles because of this.

2. Outrage and anxiety

Outrage is related with disdain, crabbiness, and anger. It can bring you anything from a headache and a sleeping disorder to comprehension issues, skin issues, respiratory failure, or even a stroke. Also, if you're a worrier, outrage can aggravate it even by reinforcing the manifestations of summed up tension issues. So as not to allow your outrage win, step back for a minute, acknowledge why you are irate, and converse with individuals about what's at the forefront of your thoughts. Discover the answer to the issue, and let go of undesirable thought patterns.

3. Depression

Depression is a mental health issue that can lead to emotional distress. This mental state increases your risk of various sicknesses and makes your immune system frail. It additionally causes sleep deprivation in view of a failure to get settled or heaps of hurt thoughts. Depression and being exposed to stress lead to the danger of heart failure. A depressed individual can also experience difficulty with their memory or deciding.

4. Dread

When you are alarmed, the blood truly drains from your face, making you pale. This happens on account of the autonomic nervous system, the fight-or-flight control system. When you face a trigger, veins squeeze off the blood flow to your face and limbs, sending more blood to your muscles and body so you will be prepared for either the flight or the fight.

5. Revulsion

Feeling nauseated by something or, far more atrocious, somebody is one of the most troublesome feelings for anyone to control. Not at all like other emotions such as dread and outrage, which make your pulse accelerate, has disgust, or revulsion made your pulse slow down a bit. You can also feel queasiness or as though something isn't right with your stomach.

This happens in light of the fact that the animosity created by revulsion has a ton of the same physiological components that make up the stomach digestive system. To stay away from this, take a full breath, understand that it's simply your emotions attempting to control your reasoning, and do something contrary to what you're feeling: rather than ridiculing a person or thing, be caring toward them.

6. Shame

In instances of healthy shame, you do not lose your confidence, free-will, and self-esteem. Unhealthy shame generally originates from the past, and, in this sense, unhealthy shame becomes a source of worry. This causes issues, such as overproduction of cortisol, the necessary stress hormone, and this can prompt a heightened pulse and constricted arteries.

To beat shame, quit comparing yourself with others. Figure out how to be sure and unafraid of what individuals say or think. Let them do what they do and say what they want to say. Remember that it's just you who knows reality. Challenge yourself, win the fight, and love yourself.

7. Pride and disdain

Absurd pride originates from adverse thoughts about other individuals together with the belief that there is nobody better than you. This association can make you stressed, which leads to acid reflux, stomachache, hypertension, and so on. The colloquialism "Pride goes before a fall" shows that being proud can prompt an outcome that ends in overlooking potential dangers.

If it's difficult for you to say, "I'm sorry," you need these tips: quit being a perfectionist, and consider your failures as an opportunity for a better attempt. Be progressively compassionate and attempt to comprehend others' emotions. Acknowledge individuals as they may be, document your expressions of remorse, and don't pay attention to shame too much because that is the primary issue that keeps us from being free.

8. Envy

A few people see envy as sweet, however, just when it's not all that much. Normal envy is the thing that an individual feels when they're stressed, or they dread losing a friend or family member. Unhealthy envy can pulverize hearts, connections, and families. The pressure of envy stimulates the pulse and raises blood pressure. You can also have different symptoms that negative emotions bring such poor appetite, huge weight reduction or addition, a sleeping disorder, stomach issues, etc.

In the first place, simply begin to believe your partner, no matter how trite it sounds. Quit comparing yourself with others, and don't mistake fantasy for the real world. These are the best tips for defeating jealousy.

9. Bliss

Bliss or happiness and great wellbeing are connected at the hip, making your heart healthier, your immune system more stable, and your life longer. It additionally causes you to beat stress. As indicated by research conducted in 2015, positive prosperity was found to beneficially affect survival, diminishing the risk of death by 18% in healthy individuals and by 2% in those with illnesses.

Taking Care of Your Emotional Wellbeing

The flow of wellbeing between the mind and body works both ways, so beyond seeing how our emotions influence our bodies, we can utilize our physical wellbeing to improve our emotional health

Fuel your body with a healthy balanced diet so you can make every second count, and abstain from smoking, and an excessive amount of liquor, which can negatively affect your emotions.

Frequent participation in exercise that you find fun or enjoy will also have various mental advantages — even a brisk 10-minute walk can improve your psychological focus, mood, and energy levels.

Probably most important of all, the act of catering for your body asserts a feeling of self-respect, which is the bedrock of emotional well-being.

Your emotional wellbeing influences how you think, feel, and act, so it's an indispensable part of your general prosperity. Taking care of the emotional side of yourself is fundamental if you are to develop an uplifting point of view, and deal with your emotions, no matter what life tosses at you.

Fortunately, this doesn't need to take a ton of time or exertion — making a couple of little changes to life can help.

Here are a few different ways to calm your emotions:

1. Go through five minutes being mindful

Figuring out how to be increasingly mindful of how you feel at the time can be an incredible method to check out your emotions. Try not to stress if your mind meanders, basically watch the thoughts, and proceed onward. With everyday practice, you'll retrain your perspective to be increasingly mindful.

2. Keep a gratitude journal

Research suggests that recognizing, or recording things that you are thankful for can improve your emotional health. Before you go to bed, write down three things that you are thankful for that day. You'll before long wind up observant of the beneficial things as you go through your daily life.

3. Take a quick walk

Being physically active is an incredible method to improve your state of mind and lessen anxiety. Capitalize on those vitality-boosting endorphins, and get outside for a stroll as regularly as possible, or attempt to discover the closest park or natural area away from the clamor and hectic-ness of the city.

4. Talk with a friend

People are social creatures. Invest energy interacting with friends, or meeting new people, so you have a solid support group of people.

5. Break out of your everyday routine

Doing the same things on a daily basis can be tedious, and leave you feeling dreary. Attempt a deviation from your schedule, regardless of whether it's taking an alternate route to work, or taking up another hobby.

6. Give something

Providing for other people, regardless of whether it's a simple grin, or a couple of hours volunteering, can help your social relationships, and improve your emotional health.

7. Start saying no

Defining limits is an important way to protect your emotional health. Abstain from overextending yourself, and if you have a feeling that you need time to energize without anyone else's presence or input, it's perfectly fine today no to things or ask that they are rescheduled.

8. Start saying yes

Then again, saying yes to great opportunities can be an extraordinary method to open yourself up to new encounters, regardless of whether it is an opportunity to take a shot at something other than what you are used to, or meet new people.

9. Do a digital cleanse

Online networking is great for staying in abreast with what's happening on the planet, yet being stuck to your phones, and seeing other individuals' highlight reels is not always good for your emotional health. Enjoy a reprieve from the social media once in a while, and receive the benefits.

10. Request help

In some cases, we need some assistance to keep our emotional health stable– and that is not something to be embarrassed about. Requesting ahelp when you need it, regardless of whether that is from a friend, a partner or an expert, is one of the most significant things you can do for your emotional health.

How to Clear Negative Emotions?

Your emotional health is dynamic, reacting to what's happening around you, your physical health, and many different things. It's alright to have high points and low points — in truth, that is absolutely normal.

Be that as it may, sometimes you will experience negative feelings that do not serve you over the long haul. Also, negative emotions can detrimentally affect your health and wellbeing. So how would you dispose of them?

Below are some different ways to clear yourself of negative emotions, so you can live the life you which to live.

1. Recognize the feeling

When you are feeling blue, do not attempt to escape the feeling, or occupy yourself by relying on unhealthy food, television, or social media. While these might numb the pain for some time, you would not have settled the issue. By recognizing and tolerating negative sentiments, you can begin to get inquisitive about what's causing them, and how you can move forward.

2. Inhale deeply

If you end up feeling furious, or baffled, or unable to sleep because of the thoughts going through your head, take a shot at breathing. Truly, something as basic as taking a couple of full breaths in and out can calm the emotions, and reduce blood pressure.

3. Enjoy a reprieve

Feeling overpowered by the job that needs to be done? Take a break. Regardless of whether you have a deadline weighing down on you, taking a couple of minutes to stroll outside, get some natural air, and gather your thoughts can assist you with coming back with restored vitality.

4. Let it out completely

An extraordinary method to discharge negative feelings is to give them a chance to come all the way out. Relinquish negative vitality with an intense dance session, or a go to the gym. Indeed, even a comfortable walk can help clear the mind.

5. Accomplish something that lights you up

Do you love to paint? Sing? Read? Invest energy with friends? If you discover negative feelings crawling into your life, take a shot at accomplishing something that you can lose all sense of direction in, and you'll before long feel more like the real you.

6. Document your emotions

Journaling can be a brilliant method to process negative thoughts. By taking a couple of minutes every day to write down your thoughts, you can begin to work through your troublesome feelings and take responsibility for your responses to them.

7. Give yourself sympathy

At long last, if life gives you an extreme hand, don't be excessively hard on yourself. Permit yourself to have the full experience of emotions. Notice what has set off the negative emotions; however, don't pass judgment on yourself for having them. Consider what you would say to a friend in a similar circumstance – and be your very own closest friend.

13. Thoughts about Calming Your Worries and Anxiety

We all have worries in our hearts and minds. We worry about putting on too much weight, how much money we have, the snowball of bills that come into our mailbox each month, and all the other things that affect our lives. Although that is a normal thing for most people, some people struggle with depression and anxiety as a result of life's worries. Their concerns severely affect their ability to function properly and do things in everyday life. This is a stumbling block to helping people get on the road to where they want to be. We are now going to talk about how to deal with life's worries and anxiety and act appropriately.

Fight or Flight

When it comes to dealing with life's problems, different people act in their own way by facing a problem or by fleeing the scene. Many people get tempted to run away from scenarios that could get them into trouble and put them into an unfortunate situation. If you can avoid such a situation, you can also flee from the stress of that situation. However, it is not always possible to avoid such situations. Sometimes you have to face the problems of your life, as Maria said in The Sound of Music. It is, therefore, best to figure out ways that you can respond to the things that are stressing you out.

One way to combat stress is to exercise. Then you can fight the worries that are clouding your mind. Exercise is one way to get rid of stress by releasing endorphins. You can feel good after one workout, which will help improve your mood and relieve you from the burdensome cares of life. Exercise will also help you feel less nervous.

The fight-or-flight response is our body's natural instinct that we can use for our benefit. It is our coping mechanism when faced with situations that are naturally difficult. Our fight-or-flight response can help us to escape situations that could be dangerous to us. For example, when a fierce animal is coming toward us, we respond by running away from the place. It is important to bear in mind that it can help us or hinder us from moving forward with our lives. But the most important thing is to learn how to face our problems.

Structured Problem-Solving

Before you deal with a problem, it is crucial that you first think of the best way to respond to the situation. When you do a simulation, you will know how you should deal with a particular situation. This will help you solve the problem. If you usually worry a lot, you will find that you will feel better after confronting your problems proactively with an understanding of the issue. This way, there will be no surprises, and you will be able to handle the situation in a positive way. Solving problems is going to help you experience greater happiness. When you know how to handle all the challenges that life throws your way, you will feel better and more confident.

Limit Your Consumption of Media

Technology has a lot of benefits for us, but it can also prove to be harmful. There's no doubt that social media can be a source of stress in our lives. We compulsively check Facebook or Instagram for the latest notifications, and then we see messages that make us worry. However, if you intentionally limit your screen time and your interactions on social media, you will find that it is liberating, and you will be free of the chains that bind you to your online profile. In addition, you will experience fewer things that distract you. This will give you more productivity in your life. Try to spend a month without the distraction of social media. Get away from it for a little while and see the difference in your overall morale. You will feel much better.

Too many of us spend over four or five hours on our phones every day. We answer messages, spend time on Facebook, surf the web, watch movies, and do other things. Consuming more media is going to lead to more stress, and therefore, we should be mindful to avoid it as much as possible. Limit your screen time to only a few hours a day; you will feel better. Read a book. Go outside and enjoy the sunshine. Take a walk. Do some recreational activities that will get you out of the house and into the world. It will feel like you've made a major upgrade to your life.

Try Meditation or Aromatherapy

When you feel burdened by the weight of everyday stresses, you might feel that there is no way to get out of it. However, you should simply find a place where you can be quiet and relaxed with some soothing music that will calm your mind. Find a place where you can allow the stress to pass away. Furthermore, you can enhance this experience by including some aromatherapy. So get some candles and scented oils that will put you in your happy place and calm your spirits. You will feel like the clouds have lifted from your mind and that the sun has come out and is shining over your heart and mind. It's a new day. Enjoy it! You deserve to be happy. Be good to yourself.

Take a Shower or Hot Bath

Another method that will help you feel loads better is if you jump into the shower or take a hot bath. You will feel that your muscles relax, and your whole body will feel a lot better. So go right ahead. Get into the water. Experience the joy of the stress being rinsed away with the water that is flowing gently against your skin. As you soak your body in the water, you can exfoliate your skin and feel the difference. You can also try aquatic therapy. Visit your local pool and allow yourself to swim the stress away. You will feel the difference, not only in your physical body but also in your mind. It is a full body experience that you will not regret doing.

Exercise

To cope with your everyday stress, it is important that you de-stress, and one of the ways to do this is through exercise. It is best to find an activity that works for you. There are many options that you can choose from. Aerobic activity is helpful to release endorphins, which will make you feel good and have a greater mood. Then you can feel the physical and mental health benefits.

If you don't want to do too much exercise, you can simply do a lot of walking. When you start to feel worried, go outside and take a walk. Even better, you can take a brief, intensive power walk or jog that will give you the freedom and mobility like you have never experienced before.

Rest and Experience Freedom like No Other

One of the things that we tend to neglect in our lives is getting enough rest. We power through the day and go on with our limitless supply of caffeine in our coffee and other energy drinks. We find ourselves spending more time on the computer. And often, we answer work-related inquiries well into the night while getting five or six hours of sleep. We just don't know how to take a load off and get away from work. That is especially the case with people who live in the United States who are prone to workaholism. We work more than ever before. We put on more weight than before and live an unhealthy lifestyle. One of the things that we need to learn how to do is rest and get more of it. It is vital that we rest and relax from all the cares of this life. Think about ways that you can do this.

1. Sleep like a baby at night.

Sleep is one of the most neglected things when life gets busy. However, we should remember that if we get more sleep, we feel healthier and happier. Getting enough rest at night is one of the ways to improve our quality of life. We can feel a lot better if we just get the right amount of shut-eye, and that usually amounts to eight to nine hours of sleep a night. I know you may be thinking, "How in the world am I going to be able to do that with my busy schedule, three kids to take care of, wife to love, etc.?"

Well, you should make sleep an important part of your wellness routine. Aside from giving you the physical benefit of feeling at your best, sleep gives us a mood boost, and we don't need to rely on as much caffeine in our system. Instead, we feel like we have more energy, and then we can go about our day with feelings of happiness. Try to get more sleep at night, and you will feel the significant change it brings to your overall health. Plus, you'll protect your body against diseases and illnesses that can easily bring you down. Sleep more for your health.

2. Go right ahead and take that nap.

Napping also has proven health benefits. Even a short 20-minute nap can boost your mood and give you the needed energy to keep going through your day. Sometimes, naps can help you recover from the effects of sleep deprivation and can improve your productivity. You can try it out and see how much better you will feel. Just don't nap too much because it might mess with your sleep cycle, making it difficult for you to fall asleep at night. Be careful but enjoy it!

3. Sometimes, it's just doing nothing.

Sometimes, rest does not involve any kind of activity. It just involves doing nothing, whether that is hanging out on the beach, swimming in a pool, taking a walk, or sitting in a given place. You can also practice meditation. Sit quietly in a given space and simply observe your surroundings. Just looking at things and staring out into space may seem like a waste of time and energy, but the thing is, resting contributes to your productivity. And you don't need to be productive every hour of the day. Instead, you should try to find moments where you can recharge your energy. Many times that is by spending time alone, especially for introverts.

4. Do some restful activities, such as walking the dog or writing in your journal.

Another thing you can do is find restful activities that don't involve too much thinking or reflection. That includes walking the dog or writing in your journal. It helps you externalize your feelings, and it makes you feel better and more energized afterward because you are not focused on the things that you must do. Instead, you choose this kind of activity. You do it because you want to, not because it's on your to-do list. It is something that will give you genuine joy, and you carry that joy with you no matter where you go.

5. Spend time with a few good friends.

Depending on your personality, socializing can either be an energizing experience or a draining one. However, most people think that it can be inherently helpful to spend time with a few good friends, playing some ball, watching a movie, or even traveling together. That can be a very restful time for everyone involved. You will see how much better you feel when you can spend a good time with your close friends. The rest will be fantastic.

14.Lack of Self Esteem

S elf-esteem is an extraordinary type of energy deep inside every one of us. It envelops that natural sense of self-worth which probably is our human claim — that sparkle that we who are either psychotherapists or instructors try to fan in those who work with us. That sparkle is just the path towards self-esteem.

It is vital that you precisely know what I mean when I state "self-esteem." There are numerous definitions that I think are deceiving, less inspiring, or less helpful than the one I present. If self-esteem loses its exact meaning and plummets to the level of a meager expression, it may not be paid attention to by those we are endeavoring to reach it — the same individuals who need it the most. There is nothing more compensating than finding how priceless, commendable, and significant you are. There is your chance to have self-esteem.

Self-esteem may be the solution to contemporary life. It is perceived as the way to monetary achievement, well-being, and individual satisfaction, and it is viewed as the remedy to failure, wrongdoing, and drug misuse. Self-esteem is, likewise, well known in scholastic circles. Like the studies of character as well as mentality research, it plays a huge part in models involving compliance, influence, psychological conflicts, physical and emotional prosperity, and social examination forms, just to give some examples.

The broad intrigue of self-esteem confirms its significance; however, this causes an unwanted outcome. Self-esteem is currently disseminated so narrowly making it hard to appreciate its true meaning. Specialists examine how high and low self-esteem is for individuals based on how they think and feel. As a result variable, a few analysts research on how different encounters influence how individuals feel about themselves), as well as interceding variable (with a requirement for high self-esteem individual is supposed to actuate an immense assortment of mental procedures).

In other words, self-esteem has turned into a shifting idea—with structure dynamically changing that it is worth may be in danger of being undermined.

In this edition, we check fundamental character, starting points, and elements of self-esteem. At this point, I may impose a question: What do we imply by the expression "self-esteem and what qualities may we relate to high self-esteem versus low self-esteem? I inspect the beginning of self-esteem. The worry here is how we perceive what encounters offer ascent to high self-esteem and which to low self-esteem. The thought of when self-esteem is significant will also be investigated, among other numerous different points of view of this critical subject.

Strangely enough, an absence of self-esteem is not relevant to the lack of skill, expertise, or capacity. It is rather increasingly associated with our discernment. Self-esteem is a method of reasoning, feeling, and acting that suggests that you acknowledge, honor, and trust yourself.

When you acknowledge yourself, you approve both the good and bad things about yourself. When you honor yourself, you treat yourself well in a similar manner that you would treat another person you honor. To trust in yourself implies that you believe you have the right to have good things throughout everyday life. It likewise means that you have certainty that you can settle on decisions and take actions that will positively affect your life.

A trait of self-esteem is realizing that you are important enough to take great care of yourself by making a sound judgment for yourself. For instance, picking nutritious nourishment for your body, working out, allowing yourself to unwind, and so on. Self-esteem does not mean you think you are preferred or more important than other individuals are, it implies that you regard and worth yourself as much as they think other individuals are preferred or more important than other individuals are, it implies that you regard and worth yourself. Self-esteem needs to originate from inside and not be subject to external sources like material belongings, your status, or endorsement from others. Having self-esteem additionally implies you do not need to put other individuals down to feel good about yourself. To put these concepts in its exact structure, I would love to offer three explanations to self-esteem as written below.

Global Self-Esteem

Regularly, the expression "self-esteem" is utilized to allude to a character point that catches how individuals perceive themselves. Analysts think this type of self-esteem, global self-esteem or characteristics self-esteem, as it is moderately persistence, both over time and over circumstances. In this publication, I have used the analogy self-esteem (with no qualifiers) when alluding to this variable.

Endeavors to characterize self-esteem have varied from an accentuation on ambition motivations, to the observation that one is a worthwhile individual of a significant universe. I adopt a quite less extraordinary strategy and characterize self-esteem regarding feelings of love for oneself. In ordinary populaces, high self-esteem is described as broad affection or passion for oneself; low self-esteem is portrayed by less positive or undecided feelings regards oneself. In exceptional cases, low self-esteem individuals detest themselves, but this sort of self-hatred happens in analytical populaces, not in ordinary.

Self-Evaluations

The title self-esteem is additionally used to allude to how individuals assess their different capacities and characteristics. For instance, an individual who questions his ability in school is occasionally said to have low academic self-esteem and an individual who supposes she is mainstream and provides a jovial company be said to have high social self-esteem.

In a comparable vein, individuals take high self-esteem at work or low self-esteem in games. The words self-confidence and self-efficacy may have been used to allude to these convictions and numerous individuals l liken self-confidence with self-esteem. I fondly call convictions self-assessments or self-appraisals, as they allude to how individuals assess or evaluate their capacities and character qualities.

Self-esteem and self-assessments are connected—individuals with high self-esteem assume they get more constructive characteristics comparing to individuals with low self-confidence do—however; these are not the same concept. An individual who lacks trust in school may love himself even more.

Then again, an individual who supposes she is appealing and prevalent probably will not like herself by any means. Unfortunately, doctors do not generally make this trait, frequently utilizing the terms self-esteem and self-assessments conversely.

The laid-back relationship amidst confidence and self-assessment is vague. Subjective models of self-esteem expect a base-up procedure. They accept that positive assessments of self specifically domains offer ascent to high self-esteem. I refer to this as a base procedure since it expects that global self-confidence develops from these more straightforward assessments.

Perceptual models of self-esteem accept a top-down procedure. Particular models expect that the occasional point goes from global self-esteem to explicit self-evaluations: Attraction to oneself in a general manner persuades people they have numerous positive traits.

Feelings of Self-Worth

Finally, the term self-confidence is utilized to allude to temporal states, especially those that emerge from a positive or negative result. This is what individuals say when they talk about encounters that support their self-esteem or undermine their self-esteem. For instance, an individual may state her self-esteem was high as it can be after getting a significant advancement, or an individual may say his self-esteem was indeed very low after a separation. These feelings are self-emotions or as the perception of self-worth. Feeling glad or satisfied with ourselves, on the productive part, or mortified and embarrassed about ourselves, on the negative part, are instances of what we mean by feelings of confidence.

Since they include sensitivity for oneself, a few analysts use the term state self-esteem to allude to the feelings we claim to be the affection of self-esteem, and characteristic self-esteem to allude to how individuals feel about themselves. These circumstances mean the same between the two concepts, suggesting that the contrast is that global self-esteem is tenacious, while feelings of self-esteem are for the short-term.

The characteristic says presumption has significant outcomes. To start with, it proposes that feeling glad for one's self is similar to gain high self-confidence and that feeling embarrassed about oneself is much the same as having low self-esteem. This, thus, drives researchers to accept that a pure feeling of high self-esteem or low self-esteem can be made by briefly pressing individuals to feel better or awful about themselves. This is regularly practiced by giving individuals positive or negative self-pertinent criticism.

Different analysts cannot help contradicting this methodology, contending that these controls do not give an appropriate match of high self-esteem or low self-esteem. Another effectiveness about sentiments of self-esteem. Several instances, in this publication, we have talked about fundamental human requisites to like ourselves. In psychology, this is referred to as self-enhancement intention. This term alludes to the way that individuals are roused of extreme self-worth. Individuals need to feel glad for themselves instead of embarrassed about themselves. They endeavor to amplify and ensure their perception of self-worth.

Hence, greater consistency and directly, we have a law of human advancement. Curiously, there is no accord on why individuals are propelled to have conclusive sentiments of self-worth. A few accept these emotions are characteristically fulfilling, immediate and necessary enrichments of our inclination. Positive attitudes of self-esteem are favored because they have come to be related to positive results, for example, acclaim from others or achievement.

Either way, it tends to be that sentiments of self-worth are wanted since they permeate existence with importance and make one's inescapable demise progressively fair. Anything the inception of this need might be, a longing to advance, preserve, and ensure positive feelings of self-esteem has been expected to spur a broad scope of human conduct. This combines action in accomplishment settings, social settings, and wellbeing settings.

15.Lack of Self-Esteem Can Cause Overthinking

Overthinking is a serious issue that affects 80% of the world's population. It's quite normal for humans to think, but when we overthink issues, events and situations, it becomes unhealthy and it drives other unhealthy things into our lives.

So, what then, are the causes of overthinking? What are the factors that trigger it's existence in we humans?

Lack of self-esteem

When you lose faith and believe in your abilities to compete against other people, you start to overthink. A person who lacks self-esteem constantly sees himself as inferior and not good enough. He/she thinks they don't deserve to be where they are. They assume people criticize them behind their back. They feel people look down on them all the time, even though the reverse may be the case. Such persons overthinks issues and may even withdraw himself/herself from the public. Then, they dissociate themselves from any form of socialization. When you lack confidence to do something, you start to imagine things. You begin to envision yourself as a failure. When you are complimented for doing something good, you feel it's a form of jest. You assume you don't have what it takes to succeed in the real world. You then, overthink and over analyze everything about you and even the people around you.

Fear

Yes! Fear causes overthinking. Fear of the unknown, fear of a particular event going south, fear of being wrong, fear of losing a loved one are all synthesis of overthinking. Overthinkers have this burning desire for perfectionism, so, they cannot accept anything less than that. Don't get it wrong, failure is never an okay thing, but people who overthink feel failure, just proves how bad they are. They don't see failure as something inevitable and something that you should learn from. When you feel that your house can be burgled at any minute, because you have experienced such incident, you start to overthink at that moment. Even when you are safe, you still feel your life is threatened, one way or the other. Fear can also be born out of irrational behaviors. So, it doesn't have to come in a pattern. Sometimes, people who live in constant fear turn to depressants and alcohol to suppress their negative thoughts. And then, they become addicts and alcoholics.

Anxiety

Being anxious isn't bad. That's one of the things that makes us humans. However, when we become excessively anxious, it becomes a problem. In this case, such a person is an overthinker. Such a person is worried about outcome of events, which leads to analyzing and over analyzing. Pressure sets in and then, you become stressed. People who overthinks feel they have to be in absolute control over everything including their futures. They can't deal with what the future holds for them, hence, they become obsessed and then, overthinks. They are afraid of negative outcomes, which cause them to contemplate instead of letting it be. Sometimes, anxiety affects their decision-making process because they think too much.

Lack of trust

Lack of trust on your person is another factor that causes overthinking and affects decision-making process. Because you are afraid of making the wrong decision, you analyze situations till you have accumulated so many options in your head. At the end of the day, you are unable to make a decision out your available options. All because of you don't trust yourself enough to move ahead. Your brain becomes bombarded with several thoughts and you become confused and mentally exhausted to even come up with a solution. You are definitely an overthinker if you go through this process.

Trauma

Be it emotional or psychological trauma, this can cause a person to overthink. For example, a victim of rape will always relive those moments when he/she was sexually raped. Such a person finds it difficult to form healthy relationships with the opposite sex, because of the experience. A traumatized individual is an overthinker and will detach him/herself from socializing with people, particularly the opposite sex.

Apart from sexual abuse, a traumatized person may be reliving the moments he/she lost a loved one. For example, the death of a spouse may make you to overthink those special moments you shared with such a person before their death. You are constantly ruminating the possibilities and scenarios of you saving such persons if you were there. You begin to raise questions about a possible scenario like this, "if I was there, probably you would have lived longer". Most times, you find it difficult to bring yourself back to the present. You find it absolutely difficult to detach yourself from your thoughts, because you feel burdened.

Depression

Depression and overthinking are like five and six. Loss and frustration, sadness, are all factors that cause depression. And when you become depressed, your behavior becomes governed by pessimistic thoughts, which gives way to overthinking and concentration problems. Depression also, gives way for drugs, food, cigarettes, and alcohol dependency. Trauma is another primary cause of depression, because you relinquish in thoughts of the past. A depressed person, sometimes suffers from derealization problems. He feels the world is unreal, flat, dull, and strange and feels detached from reality.

Finances

If you are low in finance, broke or you realized you lost an investment to scam sites, chances are that you are likely to drink away your problems in a bar and think too much. Most people recover from this though, while others dwell in their loss and predicament for entirety.

Obsession

Worrying incessantly about a person's welfare is known as obsession. Why it is normal to worry and care for a loved one or something, being obsessive about such persons or something is unhealthy and that causes you to think too much. Even when the person you care for is right beside you, you assume that when such a person leaves, something might happen to him/her. Obsessive people often develop one type of anxiety disorder because they see themselves immersing in overthinking every time.

Definitions for Self Esteem

Psychologists that have studied the concept of self-esteem have come up with different examples to define it to the average human. These definitions shed new light on the concept of self-esteem and just shine upon us the importance that it hosts. A low self-esteem can have different repercussions and high self-esteem can have different benefits, these definitions define how you can benefit or lose out through the levels of self-esteem you have.

The first definition of self-esteem we are studying was first proposed by Glenn Schiraldi as part of the Self-Esteem Workbook. This definition has much to do with the appreciation a person has for themselves. Schiraldi believed that self-esteem was all about having a realistic and appreciative opinion of yourself. The opinion should be realistic because as important as it is to not undermine your abilities, you shouldn't also have high expectations of what you consider yourself capable to do.

Having high expectations from oneself can be a bit too risky, as you can end up disappointing yourself and the people around you. Schiraldi believed that the opinion of oneself should be appreciative because that is exactly what goes on to define the self-esteem that people have in them. Self-esteem is all about appreciating the things you do and building upon them to keep repeating the success that you achieve. You surely cannot work towards success in the best manner possible, without appreciating your talents and working towards further bettering them. Schiraldi used the word appreciative to imply that you should have positive feelings and optimism towards yourself and should have a certain bit of liking towards your abilities as well.

The second definition we study was proposed by renowned psychologist David Burns. Burns positioned self-esteem at an extremely high pedestal, because of how he believed it could influence the human body and mind. Burns was himself a prominent psychologist and had worked with multiple individuals before he came up with this understanding. Burns realized that self-esteem was one of the most important factors helping people towards achieving the success they craved in life. It is said that believes and evaluations you hold about yourself will go on to determine what you become in your life. You cannot seriously have zero belief in yourself and expect good results to come by. To make sure that you achieve success, you should have full belief in your abilities and should focus on the end goal that you have in your mind.

The third definition of self-esteem that we study was proposed by Stanley Coopersmith. Coopersmith was another prominent psychologist and knew a fair deal about self-esteem and how it could motivate people into achieving the goals that they have in mind. Coopersmith was good at the art of psychology and mentioned that humans can use their self-esteem for their good. Coopersmith mentioned that the self-esteem you have is basically a personal judgment or analysis for expressing your worthiness towards your attitude. According to him, your self-esteem is an attitude that you show based on the worthiness that you hold about yourself. The attitude can turn deplorable if you don't consider yourself worthy enough, while the same attitude can turn into a benefit for you if you go on to achieve what comes with it.

These three are the major definitions that we have seen concerning self-esteem in the world of psychology. These definitions define self-esteem to us and put into perspective three different facets or faces of how self-esteem can be looked at.

Now is a time for a bit of self-reflection to absorb what you have just studied. Your internal self-esteem is all about understanding your flaws and working on them to better them. You should look to better your flaws by understanding your self-esteem and what comes within it.

The following questions will help you in self-reflecting in an advisable manner and achieving the results we would want you to achieve through this process.

- What have you noticed about self-esteem through the definitions above? Do you think that the definitions are in line with the judgments or the perception you had about self-esteem back in the day?

- Do these definitions we have studied differ from the definitions you had in mind related to the self-esteem of a human? If they do differ, do you think the difference is a minute one or something that you should study in detail?

- Based on all your ideas and definitions of self-esteem and the explanations you have just read; how would you define self-esteem in your words? What does self-esteem mean to you, in your own words?

- Do you think that you have a stable self-esteem, or is it fluctuating all the time? People often think they have multiple self-esteems, based on how their mood is. A positive mood can lead to optimism and high self-esteem, while a negative mood can more often than not lead to dwindling self-esteem, where you don't happen to have a lot of ideas about what you are doing with your life and pessimism creeps over you.

Healthy Self-Esteem

Your self-esteem can become healthy for you if it is developed and crafted the right way. Before we go on rambling about the benefits of healthy self-esteem, we first need to discuss what a healthy self-esteem is.

A healthy self-esteem is something that happens when a person values themselves and likes themselves for who they are. The idea of healthy self-esteem comes with the idea that you are a worthy being and have some kind of role to play in how this universe works. A healthy self-esteem includes realizing that humans are fallible and have different characteristics. Humans make mistakes; in fact, making mistakes is what makes you human. You need to realize that there is no harm in erring at one time or the other. Everyone makes mistakes and you to make certain mistakes in your life. A person with a healthy self-esteem happens to be their own best friend, which is why they realize that making mistakes does not necessarily make them a bad person. It just makes them human.

People with low self-esteem take making mistakes as a sign of their uselessness. Every single mistake they make is followed by sessions of over-thinking where they dissect the mistake and hate themselves further for erring in judgment. The end conclusion after these hours of thinking is that they happen to be useless and bad for making that small mistake.

A person with a healthy self-esteem realizes that making mistakes is not a crime. And, they also realize how important it is for them to be their own best friend. Befriending yourself is part of a healthy self-esteem. When you befriend yourself, you realize that you can err. You can make errors. And, when you realize that you can make errors, you also realize how to keep loving yourself throughout these errors. A person with a healthy self-esteem has high regard and self-respect, just as you would do for a friend, only that the regard and love are now used for oneself.

People with high self-esteem do not like degrading themselves when talking to someone else. They realize that the conversation is temporary and that their love and friendship with their bodies would continue for the time to come. People who don't have a healthy self-esteem degrade and pull jokes on themselves in a conversation. These jokes end up ruining their self-confidence in the long run.

Self-esteem is an important part of our life based on how much it affects us. Self-esteem is the filter through which we react to everything that we are experiencing and everything that happens to us. You can let your low self-esteem get to your mind or can work on it to improve it and make it healthy for your future success. Remember that the first prerequisite of building healthy self-esteem is to love yourself and befriend yourself.

Why Is Self-Esteem Important?

While we have listed down the different definitions of self-esteem and the healthy aspect related to having good self-esteem, it is now time to shed some light on the importance of self-esteem.

By now, you must also be wondering about the importance of self-esteem in the context of our lives. Having high self-esteem is increasingly healthy and important for you because of the benefits it hosts and how it saves you from the downsides of having low self-esteem.

People with low self-esteem happen to have numerous mental and physical repercussions as a result of their attitude. People who have low self-esteem can develop mental illnesses such as anxiety and depression as part of this attitude. Mental illnesses and problems usually start when a person doesn't value themselves and the value they add to this world.

You are the best version of yourself and nobody else can top that. The sooner you realize this the better it is for you. People who have a hard time appreciating themselves for who they are and what they do, happen to live life within their bubble of low self-esteem. The issues begin when you first start questioning something related to you; something natural. It could be your height, your physical characteristics or your voice. You start wishful thinking and hope that you can rid yourself of that certain characteristic. That is when you enter an area of no return and start delving into the subjugated world of wishful thinking. Positive self-esteem, on the flip side, includes accepting yourself for who you are. You accept yourself for what you bring to the table and don't want it to be any different.

Once you start undervaluing yourself, you would start seeing a fall in the performance that you would want to give around you. A wide range of problems take birth when you start undervaluing yourself. These problems include negative thinking, disordered eating habits, abuse, unhealthy relationship pattern, poor body image, underachievement in professional or academic life and impaired communication skills.

The image you have of yourself is what can save you from falling deep into the pits of what we have mentioned or talked about above. You can consider your self-esteem as the roots of the tree of life. Your roots define how hard or balanced you stand in your life. If your roots are based on a weakened and flawed sense of self, then you will never be able to grow to the limits you have in mind. Stunted mental growth is also a result of low self-esteem; you never achieve the kind of mental growth you want. Albeit, when you base your life on a positive self-esteem, you make sure that your roots remain firm and resilient. While low self-esteem can fluster and shaken you, high self-esteem can save you from complete annihilation or failure in life.

Difference between Self-Confidence and Self-Esteem

You must have gone through the lines above and must be thinking that self-esteem is a lot like the definition of self-confidence you have in your mind. There are some minute but distinguishable differences between the concept of self-confidence and self-esteem. These concepts indulge in the ability or worthiness of your mind, but they have a greater meaning attached to them.

Self-confidence is the confidence or the judgment that you have in your abilities. You know you can do something, but how confident you are about that thing defines your self-confidence. You can have a lot of confidence in some areas of life but can lack confidence in other areas of life. For instance, a student might think that they are very good at debating, but poor at sports. Now, when they enter the debating arena their confidence might be sky high and their oomph will be completely different. But, when they enter the sports field, all the self-confidence will fall down, and they will be back to ground one. For instance, the same student can have a lot of confidence while handling math but could lack that confidence in spellings. See, you can have confidence in some of your abilities while lack of confidence in the other abilities at the same time. While you still may be confident about some abilities, you can generally be categorized for having low self-esteem because of your attitude to your worthiness. Moving on, our confidence in our abilities is something that fluctuates. As we have illustrated and defined above, you can have different levels of confidence in different abilities. The level of confidence in a particular ability could be based on how confident you feel when doing that activity. On the contrary, self-esteem tends to be a more constant figure. Your self-esteem while doing Task A would be the same as your self-esteem for doing Task B. When it comes to self-esteem, you're thinking of yourself as a whole figure, you're not just taking one or two abilities into perspective. Once you think yourself as a whole, your confidence in a couple of activities makes no difference. If your general attitude to your worthiness isn't anything to write home about, then you will generally be considered low on self-esteem. Additionally, we can also say that self-confidence is an easier attribute or attitude to build than self-esteem. All it takes to build your self-confidence in a particular ability is to practice it, again and again, hoping that you will make certain improvements. But, with self-esteem, you have to change your greater outlook to life. There is a certain amount of inter-play as well between both the concepts of self-esteem and self-confidence. It is usually believed that someone with low self-esteem will most definitely have low self-confidence while doing most of the tasks. Your self-confidence in your tasks is based on your actual ability to do that task and your perception of that ability. While you might be fully able to do something, your low self-esteem can push your confidence for doing that particular task down. However, most people with low self-esteem happen to have a couple of tasks or activities where their self-confidence can rocket to the sky. Keeping this in mind, the concept of self-confidence is treated separately to that of self-esteem.

16. The Importance of Self-love for Your Life

What is self-love?

Self-love is essentially the regard which someone has for themselves, basically the kind of feeling and the affection that you share for yourself. In order to help you ascertain whether or not you love yourself and if it is ample, I am going to share a questionnaire with you. It's worth noting at this point that there isn't one person on this planet who is completely and utterly in love with themselves, and that is probably a good thing – there is a fine line between loving yourself in the most natural and healthy way, and loving yourself in an arrogant way; every single person has something about themselves which they don't like, and whilst that is normal, it's important to balance all of that out with the things you love about yourself too, e.g. your shining plus points.

Your job here is to dutifully and honestly answer the different questions, as this short survey will act like a real assessment of how much you truly love yourself and the kind of improvement that you really need. If you can identify your trouble hotspots, you can get to work on them much easier than if you have no clue where to start.

- Do you hold yourself responsible for the troubles you often face?

- Do you loathe who you are as a person?

- Do you regret who you are?

- If you were given a chance to be born again, would you like to be born as yourself?

- What is your definition of self-love?

140

- Do you tend to love other ways more than how you love yourself?

- Do you suffer from body image issues?

- Are you short on confidence?

- Do you take good care of yourself?

- Do you approve of yourself? Is the approval of others more important to you?

- Do you give yourself credit when you do well?

- Does the thought of failure make you feel less worthy?

- How would you rate your self-esteem?

- In terms of priority, how far down the list do you place yourself?

- Do you do everything for other people, and not much for yourself?

- Have any of your past relationships been extremely successful? If not, why not?

- How many things about your personality do you love?

- How many things about your appearance do you love?

- If someone gives you a compliment, do you take it, or do you bat back with a deflecting comment? E.g., if someone says, "oh you look really slim in that dress", do you say "thanks", or do you say, "oh it's because it's black, black is slimming"?

- Do others treat you the way you wish they would?

These are some questions which will give you a fair idea of whether or not you love your own self. You do not need me to explain to you what the answers mean, because these are part of your personal journey;

generally speaking, negative is bad, and positive is good, you don't need to be a brain surgeon to figure that out. The questions in themselves are self-explanatory and they will help you have a clear idea regarding how much work needs to be put in for the sake of loving who you are as a person. This is a journey which is worth every single step, so make sure you do it justice and be as honest as you can be, even if it is down to being painfully honest.

Basically, self-love is mainly pertaining to being honest about who you are and to be happy with your choices. You should not loathe your own personality, you should be accepting of who you are and with the right kind of changes, you will be able to enjoy your personality, and allow others to appreciate it too.

Self-Ranking and Self Love

It is quite natural for human beings to rank themselves based on many factors. In the modern world, a sense of competitiveness is often seen as a path to doing well. When you perceive yourself as low on the social hierarchy, self-love suffers. Nobody wants to feel that they are inferior or worth less than other people. When we make the mistake of ranking ourselves on a low level, it sabotages your sense of self love.

However, this innate instinct to compare we to one another can help or hinder, depending on the context. Often, we rank ourselves based on our professions, economic statuses, looks and appearance, and a number of achievements in a broad amount of areas, among many factors. In the animal kingdom, ranking determines the leader of the pack, the chosen hunters and gatherers, the outcasts, and even the servants among the masses of different species on Earth.

When people also say that they have poor self-worth or low self-esteem because it implies that you can move higher on the ladder of self-love. Although accomplishments in these areas can help boost one's ego, it should never be the lifeline source of your self-love.

Why do you need self-love?

Now that you know what self-love is, the following thing you need to be familiar with is the importance of self-love. Until and unless, you have a clear understanding of why self-love is so important, you will not be willing to put in too much effort for the sake of loving yourself, after all, if you don't understand the point of something, you're really not going to give it 100% time and effort.

It is for this reason that I am going to talk about some of the key reasons as to why you need to indulge in self-love. When you will have the right reasons to follow, it will give you the incentives that are going to guide you in an apt manner towards the destination we are aiming for.

1.   Improve your confidence

When you are willing to love who you are, it will give you the right confidence to excel. There are a lot of different challenges which life will throw in your way. In order to make sure that you can handle these challenges in an apt manner, you will have to be confident in yourself and in your ability. Confidence doesn't have to be about arrogance, gentle confidence is about being sure in yourself, and this shines through to other people, be it in a relationship, a friendship, or in a working situation. A confident person is happier person, and a happier person is a more attractive person overall.

Confidence arises from loving yourself. When you are happy with who you are as a person and you love yourself, you will be a whole lot more confident in your abilities. Confidence is needed in all walks of life and by choosing to love yourself, you will be able to enjoy the benefits of confidence in the long run. It's right that many situations in life can knock our confidence down a little, and this is perfectly normal, but it should only be a short-term process which is recovered from after a little time.

2. Feel better

It is important that people come to understand the fact that beauty comes in all shapes and sizes. There are so many people who are battling body issues day in and day out. They are so stressed about their own body type that it becomes really hard to love their own body. This is why you need to learn how to love yourself and you will begin to feel the change.

Modern day media doesn't help us in this regard, we are constantly being bombarded with pictures of the 'perfect' beach body, or the 'perfect' size 10 figure, but the bottom line is that nobody is perfect, and those images you seen in magazines and on the TV have probably been airbrushed to within an inch of their life! On top of this, just because someone has a so-called 'perfect' body, it doesn't mean they are happy with who they are on the inside – you never know how someone is feeling or what they are going through until you have walked in their shoes. Avoid comparisons at all costs!

3. Better productivity

There is no doubt about the fact that when you choose to love yourself, you will find better productivity. Those who are comfortable in their own skin are likely to offer full focus and concentration to their work and this, in turn, can help them enjoy improved and better productivity.

Look at it this way, if you are hampered down with confidence issues, body issues, self-esteem issues, and you basically don't like yourself very much, are you going to wake up every day with a spring in your step and a will to tick off every item on your to do list? Probably not. If you can learn to love yourself then you are happier, and happier people are focused, productive, and they achieve success in various parts of their lives.

4.   Harmonious life

There are too many people who are battling issues of self-destruction and depression. When you can love yourself, you will feel how harmonious life will be. These little changes can trigger the right kind of reaction in your body and this is likely to bring in the much-needed difference as well. We all need peace and harmony and in order to attain that, you will have to look out for ways by which your inner mind is at peace. This is why you need to ensure that you can fall in love with yourself.

Feeling content is a wonderful feeling; you don't have to a high-powered entrepreneur to be successful; you can simply be happy in your own life and in your own skin, and feeling content is a harmonious way to live. Battling issues in your own mind about how you feel, as well as trying to fight with your emotions every single hour, does not make you feel balanced or happy, however if you can attain a level of self-love, you won't have these issues to fight.

5.   Happiness

In the end, we all know how each one of us craves for happiness. If you cannot enjoy happiness in your life, nothing is ever going to work out and this will create a lot of ruckus for you. Put simply, you have to choose happiness, because it isn't going to fall into your lap without a little work and a change of mindset. Happiness emanates from your inner-self and you have to make sure that you can love your own self in order to give you the best possible chance to feel happy overall.

When you are in love with who you are, it will help you choose happiness and this, in turn, can bring you a lot of joy as well. No individual can be happy unless they are pleased with who they are as a person, otherwise those dangerous comparisons can come into play, which breeds negative emotions, such as anger, greed, jealousy, and unhappiness. This is not a pleasant or helpful road to go down.

6. Self-Approval

When you have a stronger sense of self live, you learn to approve of yourself. What used to bother you and make you feel uneasy evaporates in the face of true self compassion and acceptance. Seeking the approval and live if others in order to make your world go around no longer becomes a priority or a prerequisite to happiness. In a world where many people forsake joy based on what others think of them, you will be free and much more illumined by the uplifting spirit of self-love. Self-love will give you a lifelong advantage and higher self-esteem that is not dependent upon the approval and praise of others.

These are some of the key incentives to put you on the right path towards achieving self-love, as well as helping you to understand the core concepts of self-love too. Until, and unless, you are willing to do your bit and you have the fire to hone your skills in the field of self-love, it will be very hard for you to grasp the lesson.

You are Not Alone

One of the most important things that you must remember on your journey to developing greater self-love is that "You are not alone". There are people all around you, some you may interact with every day, and others that you may simply pass by, who are struggling to love themselves more and treat themselves as worthy individuals deserving of happiness.

Interestingly, when two individuals who lack self-love enter into a closer relationship of any kind (romantic, social, and business) those feelings of inadequacy tend to seep out and affect circumstances. Spouses that do not love themselves may find it hard to show affection and are more likely to argue or become angry when the other person doesn't meet their expectations in any way. In the workplace, employees who lack self-love may underperform regularly, or choose to doggedly undermine and compete with others to validate themselves through success. In a social environment, friends and associates with a lack of self-love may constantly seek approval from each other to lift and strengthen their secretly bruised egos.

This can be a difficult concept to understand when you are engrossed in your own feelings, but if you can grasp it, you can change your entire life and positively affect the lives of others.

It all starts by learning to love yourself.

At the end of the day, you must realize that there is no escaping yourself. You can change the way you look, alter your environment, raise your socioeconomic status or income, and even trade in your old buddies for a new crowd, but you will still have to live with yourself.

There is no escaping You as long as you are alive. Learning to have self-love and compassion is something that takes time to build, especially if you have judged yourself harshly or accepted the negative words and ridicule of others as law. Fear not, for you can annihilate the negative words and imprints of others from the past to start loving yourself today and creating a future that supports your wellbeing and essence in every way possible.

So, my advice to you before proceeding further is to first make your mind up that you really need to indulge in self-love. You have to understand that until and unless, your desire to love your own self is intact, nothing is going to happen. If, however you are determined and you put in the work, determined to overcome your own obstacles, there really does lie a pot of gold at the end of that metaphorical rainbow.

It isn't rocket science, although learning to change your mind-set can feel difficult at the start. Having said that, with some simple tips we will be listing here, you will be able to hone your skills and you should succeed in loving yourself lot more than what you are used to doing.

17. "If you want it, you'll take it": The Importance of Positive Thinking and Setting Goals

Self-talk is literally the ability to talk to oneself. We engage in self-talk every day; from the thoughts we have inside our minds to the stories we tell ourselves.

All of life can be seen as a conversation, as stories. A story is essentially any belief, thought, or reality we tell ourselves is real. All of reality and the universe itself is an interweaving mix of stories, both individual and collective. In this respect, the mind is an incredibly powerful tool and can be seen as the root of everything. All problems, extraordinary creations, worries and concerns, genius ideas, fears and insecurities, and solutions stem from the mind. We, therefore, have the power to create, shape, and destroy through the power of our thoughts alone.

When we refer to creating, shaping, and destroying, there are some profound implications. The power to create is a gift, a blessing; the whole of life is an act of creation. Our minds being tools for doing so shows just how special we are. The ability to shape suggests we can literally restructure the world around us with our thoughts, beliefs, intentions, perceptions, and impressions. There is great power in self-talk reshaping and restructuring our environments. Finally, the power to destroy or destruct teaches us just how essential it is to engage in positive, healthy, and healing self-talk and thinking, not just for ourselves but for others.

What do we mean when we say healing? Well, it is rather simple! All of life involves duality: light and dark, day and night, creation and destruction. Everything can be seen to exist in a state of balance, equilibrium, and wholeness. The planet herself aims to retain wholeness as she is one living, conscious entity, all of the different parts interacting to make up the whole. Simultaneously our bodies are designed to achieve and maintain homeostasis, a state of balance, health, and equilibrium. In this respect, it can be suggested that the planet, our own bodies, and all of life itself are in a constant state of healing, forever seeking to achieve and maintain wholeness.

Our minds are the tools for doing so. The mind is a powerful thing, and daily life can either be heaven or hell based on the stories, the self-talk we tell ourselves. If our thoughts have such a powerful influence on not only our inner world but our outer worlds, this suggests that harnessing the force of self-talk and positive thinking could be one of the most important, beneficial, and self- loving things we do for ourselves.

How to Think Positively

Thinking positively is very similar to self-talk, although not identical. Just as self-talk is the conversations, we have with ourselves, thinking positively, or positive thinking, is the energy, direction, and focus we give our conversations. Now, at this stage, it is important to note that thinking positively is not synergistic with being happy or joyful all the time. There are many cases in life where one needs or wants to think positively when their feelings, inner world, or some external situation may actually be very painful, sad, or neutral. Having a positive mindset, or engaging in positive thinking, is the ability to apply a positive and optimistic outlook to any situation in life with the intention of bettering oneself, another, or some situation or scenario. Applying positive thinking to self-talk, therefore, can have some wonderful effects.

Combining positive thinking with the stories we tell ourselves can improve all aspects of life. Relationships, both intimate and platonic, work, health and vitality, focus and concentration, abilities and mindset, passion and excitement for life, and the openness to learn and engage in personal projects, dreams, and ambitions are all areas that can be enhanced greatly with positive self-talk. As the self is a complex, interactive, holistic, and rather extraordinary thing, applying positive thinking and mental patterns is something that will benefit us greatly.

So how do we think positively? Well, as already shared, thinking positively is not all about rainbows and unicorns. Positive thinking is accepting and embracing the shadow, those dark or less favorable aspects of both self and life and choosing to focus on one's positives. The key is being conscious.

A choice is a very important factor when reshaping and restructuring thoughts. When we choose to think positively, we are literally restructuring, recalibrating, and reshaping our brains, the neurons inside and the mental thought patterns and programs that affect daily life. Our thoughts, as you are aware, have a profound influence on everything, both our inner world and internal health and our outer environment. So, shifting perspectives to ones more in alignment and harmony with a reality rooted in love, positivity, unity, connection, abundance, bliss, new opportunities and experiences, and anything and everything else associated with a positive, healthy mindset actively influences the focus of our awareness.

The best analogy to use is to imagine a spotlight. Picture the universe, the sky and stars at night, and equate it with consciousness (the unconscious mind, subconscious mind, and conscious mind: all of consciousness and thought). Now visualize shining a torch into the night sky with a focused intention of lighting up one specific star, planet, or faraway galaxy. The light is your intention and focus.

You are still aware that all of the other stars, planets, and galaxies exist, but in that moment of shining your light directly on one object, thing, or place, your mind became attuned to it. Your awareness shifted, and everything else in the sky, all of the other elements of consciousness, of the universe, ceased to exist. They, of course, were still always there, but the point is that in those moments of directed awareness and intended focus, the only thing that had all your energy and mental concentration was the thing you chose to shine your light on. You were intentionally lighting up something.

This is essentially what happens when we choose consciously to engage in positive thinking. The darkness and all other elements of existence are still there and exist; it is just our focus that actively and consciously has a profound effect on whatever we are shining our light at or on. This can be seen to be the fundamental essence of thinking positively: that there will always be light and dark, shine and shadow, but we always have the choice to shine the light. Our minds have the power to illuminate.

Positive thinking can be achieved through many methods, including neurolinguistics programming, meditation and mindfulness, mantras and affirmations, cognitive shaping, certain forms of sound therapy such as binaural beats, and self-hypnosis/positive self-talk.

Setting Your Goals

Benefits of Goal Setting

Goal setting does more than increasing a person's chance of success. Here's a look at why you should set goals:

- Faster movement toward your goal- Do you ever feel as if you are sleepwalking through life? This feeling is common for many people, as they work hard and still do not achieve what they want. Students finish college with a degree, but still do not know what they want to do as a career. Adults settle into jobs outside of their dream career, mostly because settling is easier. The reason they do not succeed is that their hard work is directionless. When you set goals, you have a clear idea of what you want. This helps you decide if an action is going to bring you closer to or farther from your goal. It helps you align your choices and make everything you do a reflection of your effort to achieve your goals. The reality is that when you are not working toward your other goals, you are working toward someone else's. Someone who gives in and cheats on their diet is working toward meeting the fast food industry's goals—lining their pockets. A person who is stuck in a dead-end job is meeting their boss' goals—to have loyal employees that work hard, even though they don't necessarily strive for more. When you start setting goals, you free yourself from the trap of living on autopilot and you gain the ability to reach goals faster. It helps you become conscious of what you are creating in your life so you can proactively work toward those things you want to become a reality for yourself.

- Knowledge of when you veer off track- Even people who are set in their goals slip up. They may mis-evaluate something or have a setback that moves them farther away from their plan. However, re-evaluation is a key element of goal setting. You should not only set goals for this week and this month, but you should also set goals for one year from now, three years from now, and even five years from now. Once you are thinking this far ahead, it becomes easier to create smaller goals that are more achievable. Once you have an actionable plan, you can set things in motion and work toward your goal. Everything in life is created twice—once in the mind and then again in the real world. If you don't use goal setting to mentally create your goals, you cannot physically create them either.

- Increased accountability- Even the people closest to you may cloud your goals with their own. Someone who has decided to spend their nights studying to further their career may be convinced to go out with their friend instead. This friend is more interested in their own goal of having fun, rather than supporting their friend in their educational endeavor.

- Greater motivation- The best goals are those that are set from a place of passion. Your goals should lead you toward the best life that you want to live. For you to want this life, you must choose goals that align with your core values and those things you want to make a reality for yourself. By setting long-term goals and re-evaluating them, you always have something greater to strive for.

- Ability to reach your highest potential- Many people do not live up to their full potential. They have unique skills and talents that go untapped. This is especially true for people who settle in life. When you assume that you have become all you are going to be, there is not necessarily a point to learn new things or focus on progress. By setting goals for what you want to achieve, you work to improve your skills and talents.

- Better ability to overcome obstacles- When you have forward motion, the bumps that you hit in the road become things you trip over on your way to your goal. Rather than staying stuck when something doesn't go your way, you know that you need to get up and keep moving toward your goal. This can help you overcome some of the most challenging times in your life.

Setting Goals to Grow Your Confidence and Self-Esteem

As you develop greater confidence and self-esteem, you are going to enhance your ability to strive for your goals. People who are confident in themselves aren't afraid to do something that is difficult or challenging in pursuit of a goal. They are confident enough to step outside of their comfort zone, as well as confident enough to know if they do fail, they will survive it and be better people because of it. Having high self-esteem also helps in the creation and achievement of goals. When you love yourself enough to embrace change and work toward improving your life, it makes a major difference in your life.

For a goal to be an effective motivator, it is generally agreed upon that goals should be SMART, meaning:

Specific- Creating a specific goal means adding details that help keep you motivated on track. It is easy for someone to say they want to lose weight and still feel upset when a month passes, and they only lose one or two pounds. This would be okay if they were only trying to lose one or two pounds by the end of the month. Since their goal was vague, however, they feel disappointed even though they have technically lost weight. Setting a specific goal is also important for creating a sense of motivation and accountability.

Measurable- Goals should be measurable in some way. This can be tricky when you are trying to measure something like self-esteem or confidence since you cannot assign a number to it. A better way to measure something like confidence or self-esteem is to set specific goals. For example, you might increase your self-confidence at work by making it your goal to speak up during the morning meeting one time. From there, you might volunteer to work with someone else on a project. To measure self-esteem, you might make it your goal to challenge negative thoughts for a full day instead of letting them rattle around in your brain. Even though you cannot assign a number, you still know that you are achieving a goal that brings you closer to growing your self-esteem and self-confidence.

Achievable- For someone lacking in confidence, one of the most detrimental things they can do is set a goal that is difficult or impossible to achieve. Imagine that someone sets the goal of losing fifty pounds within a month. To reach this, they would have to lose more than a pound a day. That would require an amount of calorie restriction and exercise that could be detrimental to their health. Additionally, when they set a goal this ambitious and fail, it discourages them from continuing on their path to achieving that weight loss. They might experience a setback or return to their old habits because they feel discouraged.

Relevant- When a goal is relevant, it means that it is reasonable and aligned with your values and passions. You will have trouble motivating yourself to do something that you do not want enough. For example, someone who puts in the work to be a doctor may find themselves struggling to apply for research grants or do work to further the field of medicine because they do not feel passionate about it. They may even struggle through medical school and their residency, as these are things that take a great deal of work and focus. It is much better to set goals for yourself that relate to your passion and where you want to go in life. Otherwise, you are wasting time doing something that you do not love—when you could be spending time reaching goals that will make you happy.

Time-bound- A goal that is time-bound is one that has a specific restriction on when you want to complete it. By setting a deadline for yourself, you are increasing the pressure and boosting motivation. Without a deadline, you may move leisurely toward your goal. This means you achieve it at a much slower rate than you would expect to.

18.Excercise to Gain Self-Esteem

N ow let us turn our attention to some physical activities that can lift our mood. Regular exercise is known to have health benefits which include preventing and managing conditions like high blood pressure, obesity, diabetes, and heart diseases. However, aside from these health benefits, exercises also have mental and emotional benefits like improving your memory, increasing your energy levels, makes you stronger and more resilient, regulate your sleep pattern, and making you feel better about yourself also known as having a healthy self-esteem.

You do not have to hit the gym every day in order to lift your mood or improve your self-esteem unless of course you enjoy going to the gym daily. Simple exercises are sufficient to improve your mood and we shall consider a few of them. But before then, let us see why exercises can have positive effects on your self-esteem.

Why Exercises Improves Your Mood and Emotions

Exercises help to release chemicals in your body which lift your mood. These chemicals known as endorphins are released by the brain when you engage in workouts. Endorphins are feel-good chemicals; they make your body to feel calm and relaxed. They also suppress hormones that can cause you to feel anxious and tensed; plus, they have a generally positive effect on your emotions.

Stress and tension can be increased by activities of cortisol and adrenaline in the body. This can lead to thoughts of worry and also have physical symptoms like indigestion, pain, muscular discomfort, and so on. Exercise temporarily takes your mind away from what is causing you the worrisome thoughts and stress. As you work out, you will discover that you have less time to fixate on stress-causing thoughts and the physical symptoms, as well as pent-up tension, tend to reduce due to the working of endorphins.

There is also a sense of accomplishment that you feel when you complete your workout goals. It makes you feel better about yourself. So, for someone who thinks and feels there are not good at anything, setting and accomplishing goals like doing 30 minutes of aerobics per day 4 times a week can gradually shift their perception about themselves. Their mind can begin to take note of actual accomplishments and start to rebuff the thought that they are not good at anything.

Although exercise alone may not be an effective way to treat depression, it does have a positive effect on lifting the mood albeit temporarily. You can use your routine exercises as a useful substitute for antidepressant medications. Engaging in 30 minutes of workout can produce effective mood-lifting result just the way medications do.

Types of Exercises to Boost Your Mood

You do not have to do a workout routine you do not enjoy because you want to improve your mood. If you don't enjoy a particular exercise, chances are that you will not feel any improvement in your mood if you engage in it. It is important that you choose something that you like to do. Starting a workout routine is fine but sticking to it is what guarantees the result you seek. Whether you are opting for aerobic exercise or anaerobic exercise, it is important to pick workout routines that you are more likely to follow through for a long time in order to continue to see significant improvement in your overall mood.

Types of Aerobic Exercises

You do not have to hit the gym every single day or engage in very high-intensity workouts to improve your mood. However, keep in mind that aerobic exercises can quickly turn into anaerobic if you perform them at very high-intensity levels.

Walking, cycling (not intense cycling), swimming, and jogging are all great and simple aerobics that can lower stress and improve your mood. But I would love to focus on simple aerobics that you can do right inside your living room.

Here are a few simple aerobics you can try at home.

Jump Rope: This exercise involves turning a rope which has handles as you repeatedly jump over the rope. Repeat these jumps for about 10 to 30 seconds before alternating it with other aerobic exercises. Gradually increase the duration of the jump rope ensuring that you do not go overboard. Doing this for about 10 minutes is a great workout. While doing this exercise, make sure that you turn the rope with your wrists. Avoid using your arms to turn the rope. Do not jump too high; only go high enough to clear the rope and make sure that you land softly.

Jogging in Place: This is jogging without leaving a spot. It is a great way to warm up before engaging in other high impact exercises. Start this by marching in a stationary position then gradually switch to jogging. When you jog, lift your feet about 2 inches off the ground and then hop from one foot to the other, all the while engaging your arms just as you would if you were in a forward motion. About 5 minutes of jogging in one place is enough to prepare you physically and emotionally to continue with other exercises or go about your day in a better mood.

Jumping Jacks: This involves jumping repeatedly with your feet wide apart while raising your arms above your head and back down again. Do these jumps for about 30 to 60 seconds and alternate them with other exercises like jump rope, mountain climbers, and jogging. 20 to 30 minutes of doing this should be enough to improve your mood. Make sure your heart is in good condition before doing this exercise. Also, note that this is rather a high impact exercise which is capable of taxing your joints.

Kickboxing: This means exactly what its name implies; kicking and punching a bag or the air. Avoid punching and kicking another person unless they are qualified fitness trainers. All you need for this exercise is to extend your legs and arms all the way as you kick and throw punches. You can keep this up for as long as is comfortable with you.

Squat Jumps: This is done by jumping as high as you can from a squat position. When you land, you go back into a squat position before repeating the jump. Do not jump on your toes; use your whole foot when jumping. Make sure that your landing is as soft as possible. Repeat this movement for between 30 to 60 seconds before alternating it with other exercises. Make sure that your knees are in good shape before attempting this. Doing squat jumps for about 5 to 10 minutes is okay.

Mountain Climbers: To practice this, get into a push-up position, and then run your knees in and out with your core tight and your back straight. You will need to plant your wrist firmly on the floor while doing this. Do this for between 30 to 60 seconds as you combine it with other aerobics. Repeat for about 10 minutes in total.

Staircase Exercise: Although you can use an actual staircase for this exercise, if you want to perform this inside your room, simply use a fitness step platform. It involves moving up and down the fitness step platform or staircase as the case may be. You can alternate this with other exercises too. Keep up the movement for about 10 minutes to increase your heart rate.

Bear Crawls: Like a bear, squat and place both hands on the floor. Walk your hands out to a push-up position, do one push-up, walk your hands back to the squat position, and then stand upright. Repeat for about 1o minutes. This may appear easy, but it can be a bit difficult to do.

Burpees: This is done by first squatting down with your hands firmly on the floor, jumping your feet backward so that you are in a plank position, jumping back in, and finally standing upright with both arms stretched above your head. Try to do this exercise for about 5 to 10 minutes. I said try because this is really difficult to do especially if you are not used to high impact exercises. But the physical and psychological benefits are really great. Use this exercise sparingly – don't push yourself with this one.

Bonus

Tai Chi and Yoga are two exercises which benefits go beyond physical health to spiritual growth. You may need special lessons to effectively use these two.

Tai Chi: This originates from ancient Chinese tradition. It is a graceful form of slow and focused body movement that is accompanied by deep breathing. It has been described as meditation in motion and also a gentle way to fight off anxiety and stress; plus, it is a great way to increase your balance and flexibility. It improves immune function and boosts the release of endorphins, the feel-good body chemicals. Although it was originally intended for self-defense, Tai Chi is now used all over the world as a form of gentle exercise.

Tai Chi is especially suitable for those (like older adults) who do not want to engage in high-impact workouts. It involves very minimal stress on the joints and muscles which makes it safe for anyone regardless of their fitness level.

To use Tai Chi, it is necessary to learn the moves and breathing techniques from a qualified Tai Chi instructor. Alternatively, you can use videos and books about Tai Chi.

Yoga: Yoga has its origin in India. It is a combination of physical postures, breathing techniques, and meditation. It can help you strengthen weak muscles, stretch your muscles, release tension, and relax your body. Like Tai Chi, it is a gentle form of workout that also has spiritual benefits.

There are yoga poses that you can probably try out but one thing to remember is that if any pose hurts, stop doing it. The goal of yoga is not to cause you physical pain but to help you release pent-up tension in your muscles. There may be some discomfort as you practice yoga but don't do anything that causes you pain. I recommend that you find a yoga class where you can be properly instructed on how to use the poses and breathing techniques.

Bottom Line

I am not suggesting that you should become a fan of exercising (although that is not such a bad idea). The focus of doing these exercises is to improve your overall mood. Always remember that keeping fit should be for the purpose of feeling good about yourself and also improving your health. Trying to compel your body to fit into society's standing of the perfect body may lead you into more self-esteem problems.

19.Improve Relationships Between Myself and Others : The Right Way to Look at Others

Help Someone Out/Give Back

Helping others and giving back to your community can get you out of your typical groups of friends and acquaint you with new individuals. A significant number of these people may progress toward becoming companions, guides, or associates. Other than fostering new connections, being liberal can have a lot of influence that benefits your present connections. At the point when your helping mentality brings about better communications with your life partner, family, and collaborators, everybody ends up benefiting from your newfound mentality.

By becoming involved with and helping different people and organizations, you feel progressively closer with other individuals. People are social creatures by nature, which means we need connections to maintain an ideal mental wellbeing. Interacting with others satisfies a need we as a whole have yet, at times, disregard. Beyond simply the one-on-one associations, the act of helping to address a greater issue or cause (like philanthropy that intends to diminish homelessness, or improve nourishment in kids living in poverty, or give more significant access to education) can make you feel like an important part of the world.

Helping other people confront their own difficulties can put yours into a clearer point of view. This is especially valid if your 'issues' are little by comparison. It's anything but difficult to take things like personal wellbeing, a safe and comfortable home, or a loving family for granted until you invest energy with individuals living in significantly troublesome circumstances. Utilize these chances to develop an appreciation and motivate you to benefit as much as possible from what you have.

After some time, that act of helping other people can assist you with acquiring a new set of skills — particularly if your activities lie outside your comfort zone. Think of activities that are beyond your comfort zone, perhaps something that you have wanted to try but you avoided due to fear of the unknown. Try to live outside of your comfort zone a bit to help others- for example, you could go to a soup kitchen in a 'bad part of town' even if you can't stand food service or do not feel comfortable in that area of town.

At the point when others begin to consider you to be somebody who's liberal and who makes a commitment past their inner comfort zone or circle, more individuals come to you with needs and rely on you to meet them. This is definitely something worth being thankful for. After some time, being viewed as a reliable 'partner' can open new opportunities that you could never have envisioned. Your self-confidence will surely increase.

Researchers have discovered that trust all by itself can be a major indicator of progress. So little successes accomplished through helping other people can expand on one another after some time to create and improve outcomes throughout your life. From a commonsense angle, helping exercises, for the most part, provide you with experiences and skills to put on your resume. This can directly add to your endeavors to get other volunteer or expert jobs. It additionally shows you're a mindful, well-rounded, balanced individual who can contribute to an assortment of situations.

So, despite everything you're thinking, whether it means removing some time from your busy calendar to help other people, the appropriate response is an enthusiastic "yes!" It's alright to start small, so don't feel overwhelmed. You can, without much of a stretch, develop your ability to help others after some time as your circumstances, limits, and capacities permit. Be that as it may, by beginning today, you can get a head start on contributing to the greater good of the world, living longer, developing your abilities, and advancing your personal satisfaction.

Surround Yourself with People Who Make You Feel Good

Those you invest the most energy with impact your mindset, how you see the world, and the desires you have of yourself. At the point when you encircle yourself with productive individuals, you're bound to receive engaging convictions and consider life to be going on for you rather than to you. Similarly, as you benefit when you surround yourself with individuals who satisfy you, you can better tolerate when those in your business or groups of friends are negative or extremist.

Do you see yourself as a determined worker, yet your colleagues and group need aspiration? Is it accurate to say that you are looking for that degree of accomplishment, yet are being kept down by people around you? Distinguishing the individuals throughout your life who are cutting you down is the initial phase in making movements to surround yourself with companions and coworkers that encourage and support you. The ideal approach to figure out who these people are is to consider how you feel after spending time with them. Do you like yourself and prepared to take on new difficulties? Or then again, do you feel irritated, uncertain of yourself, and not responsible for your feelings?

We just have control of ourselves and our own craving for development and change. Some portion of that development and change is choosing the sort of individual we allow in our lives, and the positive effect they can have on us. Helpful and supportive and selfless individuals are real, more so on the grounds that they don't just think about themselves, yet they care about you too. It is essential to them, as much as it is critical to yourself, that you like yourself or that your objectives are met.

Being around this kind of organization will rouse you to avoid descending spirals and ideally convince you to settle on great and sound choices throughout everyday life. Life is tied in with pushing ahead, and it's fundamental to be around the individuals who assist us with navigating towards progress. Having a constructive individual in your life brings comfort. On the off chance that you ever need a source of genuine sympathy, you will realize who to go to. Rather than holding you sad, they will attempt to inspire you, regardless of whether it's simply listening attentively or helping up the state of mind a piece.

Regardless of the amount we need somebody to change, realize they have to modify their own conduct; no one but themselves can settle on the choice to make any modifications in their lives. It harms us to see individuals act naturally self-destructive, yet they should see that what they are doing isn't working and that they have to search for better options. It could be contended that we are damaging ourselves by keeping them in our lives over individuals who lift us up.

We have to realize that we didn't deserve the poor treatment of lethal individuals and that the best thing we can accomplish for ourselves is to proceed onward and truly know in our souls that we deserve better. At the point when we realize we deserve better, we will, in general, draw in better and more advantageous individuals.

You realize who treats you poorly, and you realize who tears you down rather than builds you up. What you may not know is the means by which to expel these harmful individuals from your life.

Individuals need to know whether it is worthy of releasing these individuals from their lives. They need some kind of consent, particularly if the individual has been in their lives for quite a while, or sometimes, they can even be a relative. The response to this inquiry is that yes, you can cut off or slowly discontinue content with anybody in your life who treats you inadequately, tears you down, and doesn't have your goals and wellbeing in mind. This is about what is most beneficial for you, and an individual's absence of eagerness to change.

There are immediate methodologies where you explain to the individual straightforwardly why you are expelling them from your life. In any case, they may not be available to hear this, and the clarification might be more for your conclusion than it is for them. This is the easiest approach; however, you need to infer for yourself if this is somebody who you can be so immediate with and that this won't backfire. A letter is another alternative, the same number of us convey what needs be said better by writing a letter and giving it directly to the person rather than attempting to speak our minds verbally in the moment. You can likewise alter your writing multiple times before completing and handing off the letter, and you can spend as much time as you need to be sure you are stating what needs to be stated.

Stop Being a People Pleaser

These are the kinds of accommodating people whose eagerness to help other people and to do the favors that are asked of them brings about the pleaser being exploited by the individuals they need to please. Companions may search them out when they need assistance with tasks or undertakings that they either can't do individually or would want to have another person do. These accommodating people are driven by a sort of charitableness, and a fair desire to be of importance to other people. With the second sort of accommodating people, be that as it may, their thought process is increasingly self-coordinated.

This sort of pleaser can be grinding to others in their diligent need to "help out" in any event even when their assistance isn't required. They do what they can to help others as an approach to procure approval and shore up insecure confidence. This individual is looking for validation through being overly caring of others. They need to be loved by others and may not understand that the very practices they are displaying are the sort that can actually frustrate and smother others and leave the pleaser feeling burnt out.

In the event that you believe you're an over-the-top accommodating person, or in the event that you have been blamed for being an accommodating person by others, you may benefit by making sense of your own motivation for doing what others ask of you, regardless of whether it's beyond what they may accomplish for you. Is it accurate to say that you are attempting to charm yourself with others, or would you simply like to be of help? Those are two completely different motivators that spring from totally different needs and past experiences.

In case you feel you're continually being relied upon to "be there" for other people and individuals appear to exploit your thoughtfulness, the most significant word in your vocabulary needs to become, "No." While it's a good thing to help others as much as possible, nobody should feel that they are at the "beck and call" of others when they need somebody to help them out.

Advise yourself that sound connections include unity—in case you're generally the person who "tries to get along," yet never gets the chance to settle on choices in a relationship, that is an uneven relationship. Also, when a relationship's example has been carved into place, it very well may be hard to update it not far off. On the off chance that you feel you're getting the short finish of the relationship, support yourself. Be prepared to share a couple of instances of the occasions when you feel you have been scammed. Likewise, be prepared to offer thoughts of how you'd like things to go moving forward. Try not to grumble in the event that you can't propose an answer to the issue.

Understand and accept that your time is just as important as another's and be as loving and caring to yourself and your very own needs as you are to those of others. Assess how you invest your energy. In the event that you see that you are not getting the things you need or it feels like you are continually putting your needs and wants second to others because of focusing too much on satisfying others, make clear boundaries for yourself and respect them. Organize your time and ensure that you deal with your own needs before addressing the necessities of others. In the event that you don't keep your very own well of prosperity filled, you will have nothing to offer to other people.

In case you're attempting to satisfy others to earn their validation, reveal to yourself that the one opinion that truly matters is your own. Going through the motions to win the approval and companionship of somebody doesn't bring about a sound relationship. We might be thankful when somebody helps us out, yet that doesn't really imply that we're going to like that individual as a companion. We additionally may not even especially regard that individual, either.

The most straightforward individuals to like are the individuals who make us feel accepted and like we can be ourselves around them. At the point when somebody is continually inquiring as to whether we need help or asking how they can support us, huge numbers of us will, in general, feel somewhat overpowered and awkward. In the event that individuals are reliably dismissing your ideas of help, at that point, perceive that you might make a decent attempt. Venture back and center more around being acknowledged for what your identity is, not exactly what you do.

Not every person that you need to please is fundamentally going to need to be satisfied by you—it's only the truth that not every person we want to like us is continually going to like us. Try not to waste energy or money on someone not worth the exertion. Try not to be hesitant to request what you are being approached to give in a relationship. The most fulfilling and strong connections are those in which unity and respect are present.

This is how you stop being a people pleaser:

- Acknowledge that you have a choice. Accommodating people frequently feel like they need to say yes when somebody asks for their assistance. Keep in mind that you generally have a choice to say no.

- At whatever point somebody approaches you for some help, it's perfectly okay to say that you will have to consider it. This offers you the chance to if you can focus on helping them. (Also significant is to approach the individual for insights concerning the dedication.)

- Ask yourself: "How upsetting is this going to be? Do I have the opportunity to do this? What am I going to surrender? How constrained am I going to feel? Am I going to be angry with this individual who's asking?" Asking yourself these questions is key on the grounds that, all the time after you have said yes or assisted, you're left pondering, "What was I thinking? I neither have the opportunity nor the skill to help."

- In the event that the individual does need an answer immediately, your programmed answer can be no. By saying no, consequently, you leave yourself an alternative to saying yes in the event that you have understood that you're available.

- Set a time limit. On the off chance that you do consent, inform that individual of how long you are going to be available. In that way, you can avoid misunderstanding.

- Set your needs. Knowing your needs and qualities causes you to put the brakes on satisfying other people. You know when you feel good saying no or saying yes. Ask yourself, "What are the most significant things to me?"

- Say "no" with conviction. "The first no to anybody is consistently the hardest," These are words of wisdom which are hard to adopt but pay off in troves. When you are able to say "no" in a firm but polite manner, you will be taking needless pressure away from yourself. After all, the need to please others can be far harder to deal with than facing people. If anything, others will come to respect you since your word has value, that is, when you commit to something, they will know that you are serious.

- Sometimes, individuals are plainly exploiting you, so it's essential to watch out for control freaks. How would you spot them? In fact, it can be hard to spot such people because they do things in a subtle manner. For example, they might feign helplessness. But deep down, what they are doing is appealing to your softer side. That way, they can take advantage of your good nature. While there is nothing wrong with being a helpful person who is looking to offer support in time of need. But the fact of the matter is that you also need to avoid having unscrupulous people take advantage of your good nature. This is hardly a selfish act; it is an act of self-care.

Utilize an assertive declaration. A few people, at first, believe that being self-assured signifies "venturing all over individuals," Rather, "self-assuredness is mostly about the association." What this means is that you are looking to foster positive relationships with those around you. At the end of the day, your ability to build healthy relationships will end rubbing off on every aspect of your life.

Try not to give a reiteration of reasons. It's enticing to need to safeguard your choice to disapprove of somebody so that they understand your reasoning. However, this really fires back at you.

20. The Opinion That Matters is Your Own: Learn to Think All by Yourself

You are an extraordinary individual! In the event that you are not helping yourself to remember that consistently, I need to help you to remember it now. You have remarkable characteristics and unique abilities and endowments that no one else on Earth has. There is just one of you, out of the considerable number of billions of individuals on Earth. You are exceptional and essential.

Presently, we will utilize the things that make you uncommon to enable you to improve your confidence. Confidence is difficult to change, however as you create certainty, that can prompt more elevated amounts of confidence. We have effectively created one method for creating certainty, by posting your qualities and shortcomings and playing to your qualities while gradually wiping out your shortcomings. Then, we will talk about how doing what you adore can likewise help improve your certainty level.

We all are great at specific exercises; they simply work out easily for us. We don't have the foggiest idea why we discover them so natural, or why others discover them troublesome, yet we have a present for them. As kids, these were typically the exercises we most appreciated taking part in. We would participate in these exercises at each chance. These exercises were our preferred things.

As we get more seasoned, nonetheless, our time turns out to be increasingly more cornered by everyday assignments that are not exactly so pleasant. We got no exceptional preparing for the greater part of the day by day undertakings that are expected of us as grown-ups, such huge numbers of us are not excellent at them. As we wind up battling to finish these undertakings and we commit errors when doing them, it very well

172

may be anything but difficult to start to accept that we are basically great at nothing.

For our following exercise, we will make another rundown. Recollect your initial youth. What were your preferred subjects in school? What games or sports did you generally appreciate? What leisure activities did you have? These were the things you were enthusiastic about when your time was generally your own. In this way, these are the things you are presumably best at.

As you are making your rundown, you should feel an aching to take an interest in a few of the exercises you have recorded. Since you never truly lost your enthusiasm for those exercises; you just quit having sufficient opportunity to do them.

Do these exercises that intrigue you! It might require some investment to recapture your degree of aptitude since it has most likely been a long while since you had the option to do these things yet keep at it. You are not endeavoring to ace these exercises; you should simply attempt to have a fabulous time. The fact of the matter is when something is fun we will in general keep at it, and when you keep at something long enough, regardless of whether there were no common capacity there, you will in the end become very talented at it. You will have the benefit of doing things that you likely previously had a characteristic tendency toward.

As you set aside a few minutes every week to appreciate these exercises, you will show signs of improvement at them. Presently, you are a grown-up. You are more insightful than you were as a youngster, so now you will have a far and away superior comprehension of the action and ought to be better at applying key reasoning.

Presently, simply watch as your feelings of anxiety relentlessly decline. You will start to locate your day by day, ordinary errands to be less irritating, and you may even locate that a portion of your recently recaptured aptitudes extend to work, family life, or whatever you wind up doing. Fun is one of the best pressure relievers there is. Simply the unadulterated delight of accomplishing something you appreciate every week causes the remainder of the week to appear to be substantially more agreeable.

You will likewise start to meet new individuals, who offer your interests. As you become increasingly talented, your degree of regard will ascend among those individuals. They will even start to appreciate you, admire you, and come to you for counsel. So, they will end up being your companions. Having positive influencers around you ought to help you to remember the important commitment you make consistently. This will expand your certainty level, and in the end your confidence.

The most significant thing to remember when doing these things that you adore is that it's anything but a challenge. Try not to contrast yourself with other individuals. You are just chipping away at improving yourself, not on crushing others. We are for the most part extraordinary and will gain ground in various regions at various rates. When you are estimating progress, don't contrast your advancement with the advancement of others; contrast your advancement today with your advancement yesterday. That is your proportion of accomplishment.

On the off chance that you have low confidence, you have likely heard quite a bit of your life how useless you are (either from yourself or from others). In any case, as you start to exceed expectations at the things that you appreciate, you will see that you are really worth a considerable amount and that other individuals hold you in a more elevated amount of regard than you would have ever envisioned.

21. Overcoming Negative Thinking

How Your Script Shapes Your Life

The 'script' of your life describes all the conversations and words that you experience throughout the day. It is the interactions you have with others, as well as the words that you share with yourself. Think about the little voice in your head that you can hear when you are running late for work or when you are preparing for an interview or presentation. Is that voice talking you up? Is it telling you that you can handle what the day has in store and helping you prioritize, or is it causing you to feel overwhelmed or anxious? Does that voice make you feel confident before going into an interview or giving a presentation, or does it leave you imagining scenarios about what might go wrong?

One of the major things that set confident, successful people apart from those who feel 'stuck' in life is the way that they talk to themselves. People who portray confidence feel it from deep within. Instead of stressing over the many responsibilities they have that day, they feel confident that they can manage. They look at the day for the potential of opportunities and moving toward achievement—whether they are making strides with a new client or just catching up on housework. They are confident in meeting their goals and accomplishing what they set out to do.

For a comparison, let's consider how someone might experience their day after a rough morning. Think about the frustration you would feel if you woke up late for work, stubbed your toe on the door, and then dropped your yogurt on the floor—and that was only before work. This is a frustrating scenario that would upset anyone—but there are two ways to follow up a rough morning. For someone who struggles with self-confidence and self-esteem, this could be the beginning of an awful day. While they are in their car, hurrying to get to work, they might find themselves thinking, "I'm so stupid. Only lazy people show up late for work. This is why my boss won't give me a promotion. I'm a failure." A confident person might feel a little defeated after their morning, but they will ultimately shake it off. Their script in the car on their way to work might include things like "It is okay, the rest of the day will be better. I know I can turn today around. I'm ready to focus. People are late sometimes—I just made a mistake."

The person who has a negative script in the example is the person who is going to struggle turning their day around. By allowing their negative thoughts to govern their thinking, they are expecting a bad day. They might jump to conclusions or label something as bad, simply because that is how their mind is programmed to think about the day. By contrast, someone who talks to themselves with self-love and instills confidence in themselves is going to turn their day around. They'll arrive at work focused and ready to do their job, even though they are running late.

What Are Automatic Negative Thoughts?

Most people are familiar with the little voice in their head that they hear through the day. It is the voice that tells them 'You've got this!' or 'Something will go wrong' before a presentation. The little voice exists in the conscious mind. This is the part of your mind that you have the most control over. It is the area where you rationalize and think things through. Often, however, the conscious mind 'hears' quick thoughts that come from nowhere. These are automatic negative thoughts (ANTs).

These thoughts that come from nowhere actually stem from the subconscious mind. The subconscious mind is like the catalog of the brain. For some people, it may be the root of problems like irrational fears, poor self-esteem, or anxiety. When you have an experience, the subconscious mind stores information about what happened, the emotions that you experienced with it, and the resulting actions. For example, someone who is bitten by a dog may not like dogs as an adult, even if they don't remember the incident. Some people may not like a specific type of dog breed, without really knowing why.

The reason people do not realize this is happening is that it takes less than a second for information to be passed through the brain. Inside the brain, there are close to a billion neurons. When you have a thought or respond to stimuli, the connection between certain neurons lights up. Think of this like a path in the woods. There are certain neurons that light up and send signals when a person is exposed to a dog if they are afraid of them. The first time this thought happens, it leaves behind a small trace. It is like flattened grass on a path. As this path is walked over again, it continues to wear down until the grass cannot grow there. Each time you have the same thought, it leaves a deeper imprint on your mind. This worn-down path can be traveled quickly. It has become a habit.

Many people experience automatic negative thinking at some point in their life. Here are some of its characteristics:

- Automatic- The thought enters your mind without being consciously processed. It seems to come from nowhere.

- Rapid- These are fleeting thoughts that disappear in a fraction of a second.

- Habitual- It is not uncommon for ANTs to be considered normal by people who struggle with them. They are habitual for the brain, so they do not always demand attention. You may not even notice them.

- Distorted- Distorted thinking describes thinking that has been twisted or altered in perspective.

- Situation-specific- People do not realize there are patterns in their thoughts until they start looking for them. ANTs commonly occur in specific situations (like when you make a mistake or are running late).

- Repetitive- ANTs have themes related to the underlying issue. They might stem from a fear or a bad experience.

- Condensed- ANTs do not always make sense to other people. They may be symbolic or use some type of cognitive shorthand.

Identifying Negative Thoughts

Before you can resolve negative thinking patterns, you must be aware of them. While reading the examples above may have helped you notice some patterns, there are strategies you can use to identify and handle negative thoughts.

- Keep a Thought Record- The thought record should be used each time you feel your emotions shift during the day, whether it is the same emotion with a different intensity or a new emotion altogether. Write down what was happening at the time, the emotion you are experiencing, and any thoughts you are having. Keep in mind that you may not always be able to drop what you are doing and write in the journal. However, it is best to make your record as soon as you can following the emotional shift.

- Direct Questioning- Asking a question has the advantage of focusing your thought. This is one of the easiest negative-thought identification methods for beginners, as it elicits a direct yes or no response. Ask yourself: Is this thought helpful? Will it help me build useful relationships or improve my life? Will this thought contribute to the person I want to be? Is it a thought I have experienced before?

Often, combining a direct questioning method with a thought journaling method produces the best results. It teaches you to question your thoughts instead of assuming they are true. This habit of questioning is not meant to make you unsure of your thoughts. Rather, it should help you identify the thoughts that you should be thinking from those that are harmful or hurtful.

If you are having trouble identifying ANTs, try reframing them. Think about the words you have used and what your mind is saying with the thoughts. Now, think about a friend being in your situation. If they were going through what you are now, would you send them the same message your ANTs are sending you? Would you tell your friend they were a loser when they were running late, or would you help them work through their stress?

Framing things in this way is especially useful for people who struggle with self-esteem. When you don't have enough self-love, you may think it's acceptable to talk to yourself in this way. Remember that you are a person deserving of love. Even if you don't believe that now, you are trying to grow into a person who is worthy of love. It is a process—and part of that process is getting in the habit of refuting these negative thoughts.

Strategies to Stop Negative Thinking

Like meditation, stopping your negative thoughts is something that will take time. Remember that for most people, the negative script they have been playing in their head has existed for most of their life. It has become automatic because it is deeply ingrained, and the mind does believe on its deepest level that it is the truth.

Fortunately, once you are aware of your negative thinking, there are many strategies you can use to stop it. Try a few of the strategies mentioned below. While it may take time to establish the habits to consistently stop ANTs, continuing to refute the ideas will eventually change the script in your head. Your subconscious will become more aware of how you have consciously been changing your response to stimuli. Over time, it will not take that same path through the neurons. You will retrain your mind and develop a new path.

Getting Perspective on Thoughts
What are thoughts? Thoughts are bits and pieces of sounds, words, language, and stories. Even though it is second nature to assume we are right, thoughts are not always accurate. You should not automatically believe your thoughts. You do not have to obey them, and you should only pay attention when they are helpful. Finally, your thoughts should never represent a threat. ANTs are discouraging and harmful in nature. They shake your self-confidence and self-esteem. Words can hurt you. However, they are just words—and you have the power to decide what you believe and flip the script, so you are supportive and loving instead of critical and judging.

Remember that the subconscious mind is not the enemy. It is doing its job. As the brain is constantly busy sending out signals around the body, helping you digest food, carry out tasks, and even pump blood through your body, it does not have time to slow down. The subconscious mind is meant to streamline your thoughts—but it only knows what it has been taught. Some life circumstances can train the subconscious mind the wrong way. This is why the subconscious may be erroneous in its thinking patterns. It is not necessarily right—it just thinks that it is.

Refuting Negative Thoughts
One of the easiest ways to stop negative thoughts is to contradict them completely. Take out your thought journal and look over some of the ANTs you have identified. Now, write down the opposite. If you told yourself, "I'm not smart enough," before a presentation, tell yourself, "I'm going to nail this." If you told yourself, "I am unattractive," tell yourself, "I am beautiful." When you contradict messages sent by your subconscious mind, you are telling it not to go down that path. You are also starting to create a new path. Over time, your mind will start to follow that new path consistently, without the need of your conscious thought to intervene.

A common problem people have when using this strategy is that they get stuck in a loop of thoughts. This happens when you are being badgered by negative thoughts, usually brought on by stressful scenarios or feeling disappointed in yourself. Practicing saying, "STOP", clearly and loudly. You can say aloud or in your head if you are in public. By stopping the thoughts and refuting them, you are taking back conscious control of your brain.

Squash the Thought

In a way, negative thoughts are unwanted bugs in your brain. They crawl around and cause distress. Now, what is one of the easiest ways to kill a bug? Squishing it. Imagine your negative thoughts as bugs crawling around on the ground. Instead of letting them sit inside your head, squash them with your foot. Stamp them out and realize that these negative thoughts are insignificant.

Name the Thought

Sometimes, stopping negative thinking patterns is as simple as identifying them. ANTs follow a script, sometimes word for word. You will hear the same stories and words in your mind over and over again until you learn to rip up that script and replace it with a new one. For example, imagine that you are interested in dating a coworker—but you lack the self-esteem and confidence to move forward in pursuing them. Whenever you see them at work, you may find yourself thinking, "I am fat. I am ugly. I am unattractive. They would never date me." Instead of letting this thought run rampant through your mind, say, "There is that 'woe-is-me' story again" or "There goes the pity card". Call yourself out on your ANTs and those thoughts that seem to play on repeat.

Know When to Ignore Emotions and When to Experience Them
Some thoughts are tied to irrational emotions. For example, feeling anger when your significant other is twenty minutes late—even before you know the situation. It is the panic and the anxiety of not knowing if they are okay that causes anger. You are not angered by the situation,

but by the time you spend panicking. However, not all the emotions you experience are irrational. It is natural to feel angry when someone lies to you about something important. You should process sadness when you have to euthanize a pet or when someone you care about passes on.

As you work to gain control over your conscious thoughts, you have to learn to identify emotions that you should process. Some emotions need to be worked through. Otherwise, they will lie under the surface and erupt at the worst times. Other emotions are best left to simmer until you are sure of them. For example, you may not want to react by leaving your significant other angry voicemails when they are just twenty minutes late. It is better to wait until you know the situation before reacting.

Observe Thoughts

Like when you are practicing meditation, it can be helpful to let your thoughts float by. Practice this when you are experiencing ANTs, too. Do not participate in thinking or give it any attention. Develop a Zen attitude and observe. You can even state, "I notice that I am having the thought…" By labeling it, you can step back and consider its impact. However, you should do this in a thoughtful way.

Observation is also a powerful tool for gaining insight. When you observe, you take yourself out of the equation. You can see things clearer when you are not experiencing the thoughts. This helps you understand the links between your thoughts, emotions, and action. Once you see the patterns, you gain insight into how they are affecting your life.

ABCs Journaling Activity

For this journaling exercise, you are going to start at C (consequences). This is the most noticeable part of your thought, as the consequences are the emotion triggered and what you feel as a result of your thought. For example, you may feel sadness, depression, hurt, guilt, anxiety, shame, jealousy, or anger. Then, rate the intensity of this feeling on a scale from 0-100%.

Once you have identified the feeling, write down the actions that resulted as well. Someone who is depressed or ashamed may become withdrawn or distance themselves from others, while someone who is feeling aggressive may use drugs to 'unwind' or yell.

From C, you are going to move to A. The A portion is the activating event or the thing that triggered the consequences. Triggers are not limited to circumstances. Some things that can trigger thoughts and feelings include images, memories, places, past, present, or future events, or physical sensations.

For step B, you are going to write down all the thoughts and beliefs that you believe to be true about the activating event. Consider what that event meant to you and how it made you feel. How did you perceive the event?

Look over your part C one more time. Then, write down things you could dispute in part D. If you can, label the thought patterns that you notice or name the erroneous thought associated with the belief.

Continuing part D make a list of the original beliefs that you established in part B. Think about the situation critically and write a realistic response to each thought on this list.

For part E, you are going to write down a plan that you can use when you are in the same scenario. You can write down a different way to manage a situation or you can think of an experiment to test an idea. As you write this plan, be specific and clear about how you want to execute your plan.

This journaling activity is best completed immediately following an incident. However, you cannot always drop everything and work through your emotions. If you are journaling when the incident is not fresh, take a few minutes to replay the scenario in your head and re-experience the emotions and thoughts that went along with it. Remember that this exercise is important for learning how to work through emotions in a new way. Even if you are feeling better hours after the incident, it is important to re-process the scenario.

22. Law of Attraction to Improve Your Life

T he Law of Attraction is the ability to attract to yourself anything that you focus on.

Based on the new thought philosophy, the Law of Attraction is the belief that what you think of is what you attract into your life.

According to the new thought philosophy, the mind and the body are vibrating energies. In Quantum Physics, we learned that the Universe is full of energy frequencies and therefore, we are made of energy.

The mind has two parts, the conscious or thinking mind and the subconscious or storage mind. Ideas and creativity come from the conscious mind. These ideas pass the conscious mind to the subconscious mind where it gets stored as information. The subconscious mind absorbs everything the conscious mind encounters.

During the cognitive development years, your mind absorbs everything you see around you. Every single event, word, thoughts, action, sound, and feeling passed from the conscious mind to the subconscious mind. The subconscious mind is like a storage tank that keeps everything stored inside. The information it stores is use as a response to any stimuli.

You know that your body is a mass of energy and your thoughts are energy, which means, that whatever you think of is made of energy. Therefore, if you think of positive thoughts, then your subconscious mind will also store positive thoughts. These positive thoughts give off a vibration of positive energy attracting a similar energy.

At this point, you are probably still not convinced so allow me to illustrate. As a child, you grew up believing that Santa Claus brings your gifts every Christmas. Our subconscious mind stored the information that every Christmas we find a gift under the Christmas tree that says it is from Santa. The program inside your subconscious mind is to believe that Christmas equates to a gift from Santa. Every year, you make a wish to Santa Claus so that he could bring your gift.

By now, you know it was not Santa putting those gifts under the tree but for a long time, you believed in Santa because inside your subconscious mind is the stored knowledge of the image and the story of Santa Claus. The program in your subconscious mind responds to the stimuli created by your conscious mind about Santa Claus by tapping in on its stored data.

Do you remember how you felt when you discovered the truth? Did it change your belief? Perhaps for some, yes, but for the majority the story remains real because until now, the tale of Santa Claus lives. That is how powerful the subconscious mind is. The subconscious mind can turn beliefs into what we perceive as truths.

Using the Law of Attraction

Now you know the power of your subconscious mind. How can you relate this to the principle of the Law of Attraction?

Your body is like a human magnet that sends out energy frequencies through your thoughts and emotions and in turn, these frequencies attract similar energy frequencies.

Have you ever experience losing a job opportunity because you failed in an interview? Have you ever thought why you failed? Go back to your subconscious mind. You go to an interview all prepped up and eager to go but once faced with the interviewer, self-doubts assail you. These doubts did not materialize in an instant. It was already there long before your interview.

Probably in the past, things happened that led you to believe you are not good enough. It happened often enough until it programs you to believe that this is the truth. A failing grade in school or someone bullied you in school could have caused you to believe that you are not worthy of anything.

In this scenario, you are allowing negative thoughts to enter your mind. These negative thoughts are triggering similar negative information in your subconscious mind. As a result, your subconscious mind will emit negative vibrations. These negative vibrations will translate into various forms like stuttering, nervous hand gestures or wobbly voice. These negative reactions will attract the same negative response, failing the interview.

Unknowingly, you are using the law of attraction to your disadvantage.

Using the Law of Attraction to your advantage

Your thoughts are the mirror images of your life. Fate or circumstances do not create your future, you do. Unfortunately, it is not easy to change the programs stored in your mind.

These limiting beliefs controlled what you can become by making a paradigm shift. Paradigms are the habits formed by the subconscious mind. These are the information rooted deep within your subconscious mind since birth.

If your paradigms are all negative, then you will only attract negative energy. Remember that the law of attraction attracts what you want to bring to yourself.

It has been a common belief that what you give out to the world will return to you tenfold. If you give to others, you will receive from others as well.

What are Law Of Attraction Exercises?

The Law of Attraction Exercises are a set of realistic tools designed to oil the wheels of the Law of Attraction principles to achieve the anticipated positive results. The Law of Attraction exercises help you to cultivate positive mentality, beliefs, positive approach, and positive models that propel you to achieve your positive ambition. The use of the exercises enhances your swiftness and precision to attract and obtain your targeted desire. The Law of Attraction resonates around the positivity level of the mind to achieve what you want. The Law of Attraction Exercises is the actionable pathway to achieving your dream and aspiration in life. They are the authentic roadmap to guide during your craving time to reach your destination. No traveler gets to his or her intended destination without knowing how to get there. A clear understanding of these exercises backed up with focus and positive energies make your dream easily achievable. No matter how efficient the engine of a gasoline-powered car may be, it will not come to life without gasoline. The Law of Attraction Exercises is the gasoline that the law relies upon to perform for the manifestation of your dream.

Benefits of Using the Law Of Attraction Exercises

There are several benefits for using the Law of Attraction Exercises. Knowing the benefits behind these exercises will make them more attractive and enticing, more particularly to achieve the best you desired for your life.

The first target of the Law of Attraction is YOU. Yes you, you, and you. The attitude of You in YOU determines what YOU achieve from the Exercises of the Law of Attraction.

Check out the benefits of the Law of Attraction Exercises as expatiated below.

The Law of Attraction exercises encourages you to create a positive mindset and focus on positive energies. They help you to eliminate negative thoughts and negative habits.

Steer you to create a positive dreamland and roadmap to achieving your dream

Exercises of the Law of Attraction help you focus on what you desire, want, or where you want to be.

The exercises help you to discover where you are at the moment and where you desire to be thereafter.

They prompt you to dispel clouds of self-doubt

Build self-confidence and self-determination

Propel you to take positive actions

It creates an aura of 'POSSIBILITY' around you with a thick field of positive energies.

They build a clear focus program that eliminates distractions for the manifestation of your dream

Helps you from unnecessary dissipating of energies on speculation, thereby focusing your real dream.

The Law of Attraction Can Transform Your Life

Your life can transform dramatically by using the Law of Attraction to your advantage.

Here are a few things how mastering the law of attraction can enhance your life:

- You learn to trust your instincts and follow your intuition. You do not overthink and instead allow your emotions to direct you on the right path.

- You can increase the power of your dreams. As your thoughts grow larger and more powerful, you can dwell and believe more in your dreams. You can get more ideas on mapping out new paths towards fulfilling your goal.

- You can take control of your thoughts and shift your focus on more positive thoughts rather than the negative ones.

- You move one step closer to fulfill your dreams. Though success requires consistent work and action, it is empowering to know that every positive thought you have moves you closer to your goal.

• Your belief about success will change. If you think success is exclusive to a privileged few, the law of attraction will show you that it is possible for everyone to achieve success.

• You will become more productive and instead of wallowing on your mistakes, you give more focus on your goals and achieving them.

• You will have more control over your future and not at the mercy of others. Your positivity affects your interpersonal relationships by attracting better bonds.

Preparing yourself

In order to reprogram your subconscious mind, you need to prepare yourself. You are going to battle with years of old habits deeply rooted in your subconscious mind.

You need to get ready in body, mind and soul.

23. Quick and Practical Self-Esteem Boosting Tips

T he secret to getting ahead is getting started." – Mark Twain

Getting started is the most important key to ever achieving anything, including a healthy self-esteem. Unfortunately, there are 2 things that cause people to fail from the get-go.

First is laziness. Some people are just too darn lazy to get anything started. Another reason is discouragement.

People get discouraged from even starting because of past failures or because the initial first steps are intimidatingly difficult. We are able to succeed at getting started by starting with small, easier steps and gradually increase the difficulty and complexity, allowing small successes to build up to bigger ones.

Here are 10 things we can do within the following ten days that can help us quickly build our self-esteem momentum that will carry us forward into long term self-esteem success:

-Day 1: Recall something that you did really well, even for the first time. By recreating the sensation and feeling of past successes, you release dopamine into your brain.

It can also help you feel more confident when doing something new. By recalling past successes, you objectively establish our ability to get things done, which can definitely boost your self-esteem.

-Day 2: Indulge in something you do really well. By doing this, you physically remind yourself that you are capable of doing things well. I love playing the guitar moments before engaging in an unfamiliar activity or learning something new as it makes me feel good about myself, which is a great way to start doing or learning something new.

-Day 3: Finish those long pending items in your to-do-list. Doing this helps you experience a sense of accomplishment that's beneficial for making you feel good about yourself. On the other hand, a growing pile of to-do-list items can hamper your self-esteem because it sends the subtle message that you can't get things done.

-Day 4: Think about others for a change. As much as low self-esteem is about thinking lowly of ourselves, we can also suffer from it by thinking too much about ourselves. When we do that, every little flaw is magnified, making depression and low self-worth mountains out of molehills. By thinking about other people for a change, you redirect your attention away from your perceived shortcomings. That can help boost your self-esteem fast.

-Day 5: Relax by getting a massage, sleeping the whole day or enjoying your favorite TV shows – whatever makes you feel rested and refreshed. Often times, being too busy and hectic makes stresses us out, making us highly strung and more sensitive to our "shortcomings" more than the usual. By relaxing, we get to breathe and give ourselves the chance to let all that stress and tension evaporate. As a result, we become less critical about ourselves and enjoy a healthier self-esteem.

-Day 6: Treat yourself to your favorite food. Trying to eat too healthy can be stressful and make us feel bad about ourselves. Often times, eating healthy is due to a desire to lose weight. By overdoing it as in the case of crash and overly restrictive diets, we run the risk of a very strong rebound of binge eating and more weight gain. By giving yourself a break, you minimize that risk and feel better about yourself.

-Day 7: Exercising, particularly aerobic exercises like running and biking release endorphins in our bodies – a happy hormone. Whenever I feel down, I love to go out for a run. It never fails to make me feel much better about myself and my particular situation at the time.

-Day 8: Buying new clothes can instantly make us feel better about ourselves, especially when we buy clothes that look really good on us. To make the most out of this, it's best that you tag a fashion expert friend along to help you pick out clothes that complement your looks.

-Day 9: Going to church can help you feel good about yourself, even if you're not a religious person. In particular, seeker-sensitive churches like Lakewood Church or Hillsong Church preach messages that are primarily meant to encourage people more than giving them a list of moral to do's and not-to-dos. If you're not a Christian or particularly religious, you can listen to or watch podcasts of the best motivational speakers.

-Day 10: Being thankful for all of our blessings regardless of our situations is one way to quickly raise self-esteem. In particular, I find it especially helpful to remember how many other people have it worse than I do, i.e., people dying from famines, people tortured and murdered for their religious beliefs and people living on the cold streets, among others. Nothing makes for a good self-esteem raise than seeing how things can be much worse and how things are much better for us compared to others.

24. How Self-Hypnosis Can Increase Our Self-Esteem and Confidence

Y ou've seen it in action or heard it talked about. You spend so much time working on bettering yourself, on watching what you eat, on exercising, on progress in your career, social status, making sure you are the absolute best you can be. You are so hard on yourself, yet you go out in the world and see all these people who have it so much easier than you, getting more with less effort. They just have a way about them. They have a genealogically inherited savvy, if not looks. What makes them so special? Why can't you be like them?

The answer is so very simple. Some call it the law of attraction, making it spiritual, saying that if you manifest the energy of what you desire to be within yourself, then that energy will attract what it is you desire to you, making you that thing that you desire to be. In deduction, positivity is attractive, and negativity is repulsive. We desire to be around people who feel good about themselves because of their affability and acceptance of life and love for the universe makes us feel good about ourselves. And, if we are positive, we desire the company of other positive individuals and very much dislike the company of negative individuals impeding on our emotional and spiritual freedom with mindless chatter and noise. If you spend all day worrying about yourself and questioning your value, how does that make the people around you feel? Do you care? Because the way you make the people around you feel is very much a part of how effective you are in socialization. Imagine the beautiful person who feels they are ugly and has no friends or companions because their own hatred and scorn for themselves reflects onto others, making them question their own beauty because how could they not be ugly when this person is so beautiful? Well, that beautiful person lives inside of us all, as we are all beautiful in our own light, the light of love. We all have something to offer, and that thing cannot be offered up uninhibitedly until we accept it for ourselves first. Beauty is absolutely in the eye of the beholder. Vain people, materialistic people who spend all day long judging everyone they see by their looks, with some predetermined and meticulously defined specific standard that is totally incidental in the fabric of the cosmos, completely defined by some culture or fad or another mode that will come and go with the tides, have no close or lasting relationships themselves, and completely fail to understand what drives human beings together in love, a failure which only further agitates their own weakness and hate to continue increasingly to label others. This is a growing, contagious culture of loneliness and negativity and beauty standards that will never be met. People in legitimate, loving relationships know that such relationships are not built on looks but on intimacy, an intimacy that is experienced mentally, physically, and spiritually. Two beautiful people do not make a loving relationship just by being two beautiful people. Two people, open and honest, ready and willing to learn together, accepting of each other's flaws as well as their own, yet willing to grow and better themselves together as a unit, make a loving relationship. As such, a relationship can be comprised of an objectively "ugly" person and an objectively "beautiful" person, depending on the circumstance as well as the perception of the voyeur. If you are out people watching and see such a relationship, realize your own fallibility in defining what is "beautiful" and what is "ugly." You may say, "she is only with him for his money," and you may be onto something. Wealth is attractive but not only material wealth but also spiritual, emotional, and mental wealth. Smart people are attractive. Funny people are attractive. Easy-going people are attractive. Loving people are attractive. People who are open-minded and not quick to judge are attractive. People that don't go around labeling others "ugly" and "beautiful" are attractive. People that don't box themselves into a certain predetermined standard of beauty are attractive, and they will attract whatever it is that they need, be it in an "ugly" or a "beautiful" person.

Knowing all this, we must stop labeling ourselves. If we have low self-esteem, we must get to the cause of our own negative labeling of ourselves. Do we feel that we are unattractive? What is it that you feel you are incapable of attracting? Because, when we love ourselves and understand our own needs and gifts, we automatically attract whatever it is that the universe feels that we need. No one is "attractive" to everyone. Everyone is "attractive" to the things that they attract. If you are negative, you will attract negativity. If you are positive, you will attract positivity. Both positivity and negativity come in many shapes, sizes, and veneers. An objectively beautiful person can be incredibly negative and only attract negativity. An objectively strange-looking person can be incredibly positive and only attract positivity. If you are negative, you will see this strange looking person on the street, and envy them, and wonder why they have so much more than you, when they are not as objectively "attractive." Maybe you can find another negative person, and the two of you can go back and forth with insults and bond over the shared labeling of another and the negative energy you try to throw at them. But know that whatever negativity you throw at a positive person will only bounce off of them and come back to hurt you tenfold, in a positive ray of light. And by hurt, I just mean that it will shed light on your own darkness, a light which might cause you to self-reflect and see yourself for what you really are, what you have really been, a negative person only attracting negativity.

So, we must stop judging ourselves in a negative light, and find the positivity in our own self-perception. We must find the beauty in ourselves, so that other people may see it in us, as well, and be attracted to it for what it offers, a sharing in the light. We must believe and know that we are attractive and that we have something to offer to the right person, whoever that person may be. And we must grant others the same and stop reveling in a negative culture of shaming. When we hate ourselves, for whatever reason, feeling ugly and insecure, we do not feel free to be ourselves. And if we are not ourselves, how can we attract what it is that our selves desire? We must open up the floodgates and be ourselves above all things and stop worrying about how we will be perceived by others. When we are who we are, nature has a way of sorting out those that we belong with and those that we do not belong with. No one can please everyone. Those who attempt to please everyone, as the story goes, end up pleasing no one. We must stop worrying about who we are pleasing and simply live to please ourselves, and, in effect, please those who belong around us, the law of attraction working its natural order, grouping people who belong around each other together and keeping those who do not belong around each other apart. In this, only worrying about being ourselves and not about being anybody else, we develop confidence. And with this confidence, we begin to attract more and more people, as it is realized all that we have to offer them. There is room for many different people to coexist symbiotically, to gain something from each other once we are open about who we are and accepting of each other's differences. We must never question if we belong because we all belong, that's why we are here. It is not your job to find where you belong—simply be yourself, love yourself, and exude confidence, and you will end up where you belong by sheer force of nature.

It can be hard for someone who is so learned in the art of judgment to eschew beauty standards and realize that there's more to a human being than first impressions. Sometimes we have gone our whole lives thinking that way, and now we must realize that we have very little to show for it but a huge stinking pool of negativity. The universe works in strange ways, and it is nearly impossible to define specific things like who has value and who does not. So, we must realize that this simply isn't up for us to define. It is something that is so ingrained in our culture; it really is a huge slap in the face once you wake up to it if you are privy. In the media, on television, in movies or magazines, so much of what is expressed to us is centered on the vanity. And, ironically, those who consume this media the most are people who are very lonely, consuming the media as some form of replacement for human connection. Thus, this negativity in the media is preaching to the choir in this way. If you wish to be negative and to judge others, know that you will have plenty of company but know that that company is not a good company, and you will have very little to show for your loyalty to it at the end of the day. It's best to turn your eye away from others and focus on yourself, and not on judging yourself, but of being forgiving towards yourself and your flaws. No one sees the flaws in us as we do. We are our own harshest critics; it comes with the territory of being the ones who spend the most time with us. We are the ones who have to deal with ourselves day in and day out, and thus it is we who have the greatest power to either be our greatest lovers or our greatest detractors. It is always better to be loving than to be hateful because it applies to everything. We must love ourselves and love others as we love ourselves.

When you are feeling insecure, really think about what it that you are feeling. How do you perceive yourself? How does what you perceive differ from what you perceive in others that you may envy? Is there some idyllic standard of beauty that has been ingrained in you by an outside source that may not have really been the one with the power to define what is beautiful and what isn't? Are they really worth taking the suggestion from to define your own self in this way? It would help to change the method of thinking. Maybe consider what someone might possibly perceive about you in a positive light. Focus not on your perceived negative attributes but find a new attribute that can be imbued with positivity. Do this, and in this new context, maybe you can begin to reexamine those perceived flaws that you would call the initial catalyst for your insecurity. Let's say you are looking in the mirror and your eyes immediately, every time, go to a blemish on your shoulder, a birthmark. Something you have that others don't, something that sets you apart from others. Begin to look somewhere else. Look at different parts of yourself that you may not have paid as much mind to before. Or just look into your eyes and smile. In your peripheral vision, that birthmark might be freed of the negative connotations you have put on it over the years of negative overthinking. That birthmark is just another part of you that makes up the whole. Any perceived flaw is just one small part of you, and we are infinitely more than the sum of our parts. Never dwell on the negativity and always be positive. Tell yourself that you are good, and you are beautiful, and, by deduction, every small part of you is beautiful in that it makes up the whole, which is beautiful. No part of you ever exists on its own without you. And you are beautiful because you exist and because you choose to love.

And while it is never wrong to take care of yourself, to exercise, to watch what you eat, to wear the clothes that you want to wear and fashion yourself and your hair to the image that you most desire to be, know that you should do these things for love and positivity, not out of fear and negativity. Don't do these things because you don't want to be ugly anymore, do them because you want to continue to be beautiful, and to be the best you that you can be, the way that you choose, as you are always changing and growing and self-improving. Love yourself for what you do and do what you love. Physical perfection isn't even half of the battle without also realizing yourself mentally and spiritually. The eyes are the windows to the soul, and when someone looks into your eyes, the way a person sees you can change drastically depending on how you are feeling at the moment, about yourself, about life, about others. A strong smile and open eyes with lots of love can go infinite ways towards making a person very beautiful, regardless of any physical or material attributes. Be the best that you can be, dress the way you want to, work towards bettering yourself, feel good about yourself and others, feel loved, and smile.

Let us examine some specific ways to put this into an application. Perform your induction into the trance-state, having prepped the goal already, that goal being to increase your self-esteem and your confidence. Now, visualize yourself, as you are. Comment to yourself that you are beautiful. Tell yourself that if anyone sees you and says that you are not beautiful, they are merely looking in a mirror and saying that they do not view themselves as beautiful. Visualize yourself smiling and happy. Tell yourself that you are attractive, you are happy and beautiful, and you will attract whatever it is you need to by continue to be your best self, being happy and free and open and accepting of yourself. Visualize yourself with another person, laughing, having a good time, and enjoying each other's company. Tell yourself that you deserve to be loved, and others enjoy being around you because they enjoy who are you. You are a positive and loving person, and you have a lot of love to give to whoever wants it, and whoever wants it will be an equally loving and positive person because that is what a loving and positive person attracts. Visualize yourself as the center of attention and everyone is looking straight at you. Tell yourself that the people who are watching you are amazed at what they see when they look at you and feel in their hearts a positivity and self-love inspired by your being. These people want to know you and want to be around you and would like to share with you what they have to offer and receive from you what you have to offer. Visualize yourself naked, lying in the grass, a totally natural extension of the Earth itself, exactly as you were meant to be, however, you are. Tell yourself that you are a manifestation of the universe, and you are beautiful and full of love. You and it are working in each other's best interest when you hold that love and positivity upfront in your daily being. Now, lastly, visualize anyone and everyone who has ever put you down and said or done things that you have remembered and held onto and used in your own definition of yourself to tell yourself that you are not an attractive person. Tell yourself that these people do not have the power to define you, and are merely afraid to define themselves; hence they are lashing out at you, blindly, imposing on you their own constrictions that they feel when they view themselves. Tell yourself that these people are envious of you, and were only trying to bring you down in their own mind by defining you as something that is less than them, so that they can feel superior to you in their own mind, to satiate their desire not to feel undefined and empty personally. Tell yourself that these people feel they are ugly first and foremost and are unloved, and it is this pain that causes them to define others in their steed, to impose on other people a definition that suits their needs to feel better about themselves in some unnatural way, that only serves to further their loneliness and isolation and inability to feel fulfilled in their daily lives, in their quest for love and their desires to be known and understood. It is hating and fear that causes others to bring you down. This hate and fear will not stand in your light and evaporates before your being because your own definition of yourself is so strong and positive that any negativity shatters before it. Tell yourself that the only reason anyone would ever try to convince you that you are unattractive is that they are trying to convince themselves that you are unattractive in a fruitless jester to deny the envy they feel when they look upon you. If you allow this false definition to impede on you, no one benefits from it. By allowing yourself to be the beautiful person that you are, you are standing for love and light and positive understanding that will wash away all fear and doubt.

25. Self Hypnosis Session

S it back. Relax. Now close your eyes and go into a relaxing state of trance. As you breathe in and out notice how that sense of relaxation begins to deepen. Feeling comfortable, peaceful and relaxed. Just paying attention to your breathing and allowing your mind and body to relax naturally in this comfortable session of hypnosis.

Just relax and find it easy to drift into deeper levels of relaxation as you listen to my voice because you are curious about all that I have to say. That's right. Just finding it easy to relax and feel totally comfortable right now.

Notice the chair and feel that you are safe as you find it easy now to continue to relax.

Notice how as you breathe in and out your relaxation can just deepen even more easily right now. Notice how easy it is to allow your eyes to relax. Then allow your jaw to relax and as you continue to breathe just allow your body to comfortably and easily relax.

That's right.

Just relax totally and completely.

As your body relaxes notice how your mind can relax in all kinds of interesting ways. Which means that you can comfortably drift deeper inside your inner world of wonderful, peaceful pleasant memories. Because I know that you are interested in all I have to say and as you are interested in my words so your mind can relax even more easily. Because you are imagining that, the relaxation occurs even more quickly, so you will find yourself even more comfortable and even more relaxed now

The more relaxed you become the deeper into hypnosis you can go, feeling calm, relaxed and safe as you just drift deeper.

There may be sounds around you and these sounds simply means that you can go deeper, more relaxed, into hypnosis. Enjoy drifting into a comfortable relaxing state as you continue to become even more relaxed. And wherever you go on this wonderful journey remember that my voice will go with you and the meaning behind my words will be clear to you.

As you continue to relax, notice how your breathing has changed and your body can become even more comfortable because you have felt comfortable before and that means it is easy for you to allow this relaxation to deepen and when you do that you drift into an even deeper sense of comfort, every time you breathe in and out that comfort and relaxation deepens.

And you could allow your unconscious mind to guide you easily through this learning state, couldn't you? Though it's not necessary for you to go into a deep state of hypnosis. There's no need for you to let go completely until you realize that it's safe for you to do so right NOW.

I have to tell you that actually you don't have to do anything at all because you're your unconscious mind that does it for you and integrates everything for you. So you don't even need to be aware of how relaxed you are NOW and you really don't need to be aware of the full access that you have to your resources and you continue to relax even more deeply into this wonderful state of hypnosis.

And how you will know that you are completely relaxed now? I wonder if you have realized that you are in fact completely and totally relaxed already. That's right, more of that. And you can continue to marvel at how wonderful this feeling of complete relaxation feels knowing that it allows you to access resources from the deepest part of your unconscious mind. Which means that you can enjoy this deep sense of relaxation and comfort.

You have a past and a future which means you are listening intently to all that I have to say because your unconscious mind can accept these suggestions easily and you can integrate them into your thoughts and behaviors at your own pace.

Maybe you didn't notice consciously that you have access to all the higher levels of self-esteem that are part of you and now you can. And that means that you can access all the confidence that is yours by right and every time that you do this you feel your real sense of worth and value increasing more and more. This sense of confidence and self-esteem is magnetic and you easy draw to you the people and events that show you that you are of value and demonstrate you are worthy and your focus on the future gives you even more confidence in that.

By focusing your mind inside, realize that you can access confidence and self-esteem at will, it is there by rights and you can feel that confidence and self-esteem increasing all the time. I'm not saying you really should notice that right now, maybe you will notice it in a moment.

Every time that you realize that you have confidence and increased levels of self-esteem notice that you feel worthy and of value because you are a valued individual. That means that you have confidence in your abilities and it's an experience that is familiar to you which allows you to know that every time you want to feel confident you know that self-esteem is there because it is indeed part of you and that confidence comes naturally to you now which makes you feel of value.

And that means that you can easily do all the things you want to do confidently because you know your worth and you know you are of value.

Because you are in hypnosis that means that when you decide to go into a trance will be will able to access deeper levels of relaxation even more quickly and even more easily.

You really are a truly amazing person with such a warm and magnetic personality which creates such a positive effect on all those people around you and who come in contact with you day to day, as you realize the changes that this journey has created for you now.

You have done a wonderful job and you are a great hypnotic subject which means that your unconscious mind has found it very easy to accept all these useful and beneficial suggestions that I have given you. All of these suggestions have been absorbed into your unconscious mind and are part of you now and you can allow them to integrate into your behavior at your own pace.

In a moment I am going to count from 1-10 and on the count of 10 you will be fully awake; your mind will be clear, and alert and you will feel wonderful in every way.

One waking up, two waking up, three waking up, four coming out of hypnosis, five waking up, six waking up, seven eyes starting to open, eight waking up, nine mind clear and alert, ten back in the room and feeling wonderful in every way.

Take your time before continuing with your day or evening.

26. Deep Sleep Hypnosis Session

This is going to be a thirty-minute guided hypnosis session to help you drift off into a deep and relaxing sleep. The most important thing to do while listening to this session is to keep an open mind. You must go with the flow, listen to my voice, and remember to breathe. Remember, it is not always possible to enter a light hypnotic state on the first try, but we are going to try as I guide you gently and smoothly into this state so you can fall asleep. Please bear in mind that you are not going to enter any sort of deep catatonic state. Nothing is going to be physically altered within the realm of your mind. The process of hypnosis and this guided meditation is extremely safe, and you are in control of it.

Now, I want you to get comfortable. Because you are trying to achieve a deep sleep, you should be lying down, your head resting on your most comfortable pillow and you are warmed by your softest blanket. Lie back and let your shoulders go slack, relaxing against the cushion of your bed. Gently close your eyes and release all the tension from your muscles. Release the tension in your arms, then your legs. Let go of the tension in your chest and in your back. All of the muscles in your body begin to feel looser and looser and your body is feeling light.

Recognize that this is a time for only you. You have set aside all of your day's activities and are now ready to fully embrace a beautiful and peaceful sleep. Breathe in this moment of relaxation, where nothing else matters. There is only you in the warmth of your bed.

As you lay, I will ask you something very simple. In your mind's eye, imagination a kind of ruler or some sort of measuring device. Imagine something which can measure the depth of your own relaxation. Imagine this ruler in the front of your mind. Perhaps it is your favorite color, smooth with small painted tick marks and numbers.

Take a moment to notice where you are on your current level of relaxation. Out of a scale of 100 down to 0 being your most relaxed state. Understand that there is no right or wrong measurement to begin with. Explore your state, be honest with yourself as you measure your relaxation. What tensions do you still have left in your body? What anxieties, sadness, or pain still lingers? Very soon you are going to increase your relaxation and melt away this negativity and drift off into a peaceful sleep.

Perhaps are currently at a 60 on your scale of relaxation. Even though you may actually be lower down than that, imagine yourself moving the marker in front of you. With each deep breath, you slide the marker further down along this ruler closer and closer towards zero, towards immense relaxation. As you breathe and the marker slides down, you feel your muscles release in your arms then your legs, your back relaxes, and your chest opens like a flower, welcoming in big and tranquil breaths.

You may be aware that your sense of relaxation has expanded inside of you. Perhaps all the way down to 40 or 30. You see the marker slowly glide downwards along the scale. You feel that a wave of warmth has washed over you and you are beginning to feel your whole body becoming engulfed in the warmth of peace. As you feel your body releasing its tension even more now, you feel calmer. You have now reached a ten on your scale and gently, you take a deep breath through your nose. Let it fill your stomach until it is like to burst. Then release it.

You reach nine…You enter a peaceful, calm environment.

You reach eight…You can feel the warmth of the sun on your face. It is a reminder that you are loved.

You reach seven…Each sound that you hear, you do not deny. Instead it lulls you further and deeper into a deep state of relaxation.

You reach six... You inhale through your nose and fill your belly. You inhale all of the good things the world has to offer.

You reach five... Gently, through your nose, you release your breath. You expel any negative feelings that remain.

You reach four... You feel your body becoming lighter. Your arms and legs feel weightless and free.

You reach three... You feel your chest brimming with warmth and light.

You reach two... You accept the peace that has enveloped you. This peace welcomes you into a deepening serenity as your mind quiets.

You reach one... You feel yourself drawn towards the warmth of peaceful sleep, so close you can almost graze it with your fingertips.

You reach zero... You feel a comfort deep within you that starts in your chest and radiates outwards like a blooming flower. This comfort fills you with security and you remember that you are safe. You have released your worries and concerns, and in its place, there is warmth, light, and comfort.

Gently you are lulled by this wave of serenity. You feel yourself beginning to drift beyond zero, into a realm of warm colors. Billows of reds and pinks, yellows and oranges undulate around you in soft embraces until you float down onto a plush, cool surface.

With only your fingertips, you detect that you have landed on a grassy field. Around you, you can smell the sweet fragrance of wildflowers that have populated this clearing. Your body and mind have quieted to listen to the soft rustle of the breeze through grass and flower petals, and you remember the beauty of the earth. You breathe in through your nose a deep breath that fills your stomach. Through your nose, you slowly release it.

You recognize the warm colors from before, now painted in the sky. The reds fade into pinks seamlessly as though crafted by a painter's brush. The hues swirl into the setting sun and exude a warmth that you feel throughout your body. You are existing in this space with only beauty. You are existing without concern for time or worry. There is only you in this space and all of the tranquility it shares with you.

The pinks give way to magentas, then onto violets and dark blues. The sun sets and reveals an endless sky, sprinkled with thousands of twinkling stars. You see dustings of silver and purple in the sky. The bright sliver of moon casts its beam upon you, cascading you in comfort.

Your muscles seem to melt, going slack and welcoming sleep. The stars above you dance, twirling through the vast stretch of sky, but you are still. You allow this positive energy to enter your mind. It swells within you until you feel peace exuding from every pore. You have reached a depth of serenity that exists on the brink of sleep. Allow yourself to accept rest.

Underneath the moon, you accept rest. Soon, you begin to notice a new pleasing sensation that arrives at your arms and spreads to your legs and your back, your neck, and forehead. You recognize this sensation as a sublime floating energy entering your body. You feel a delicate tingle throughout your body, ushering in lightness and calmness. This sensation is like a soft white linen, cleansing you from the inside out. It is a warm touch of healing energy, of love and passion.

These soft vibrations rid you of tension. Anxieties are expelled. Sadness and fear no longer exist here. All of the leftover stress is now dissolving entirely, turning into dust carried off by the wind. It is melting away under the power of this healing energy. In its place there is safety and the knowledge that you are loved by whom you love. It is merely you, the stars, and the moon.

The lightness you feel swells, as if tiny balloons are attached to different parts of your body. You feel your body beginning to rise and drift upwards in the direction of the stars. Peacefulness and serenity are lifting you higher into the air into the welcoming embrace of the expansive night sky. For a brief moment you understand that you exist in the space between the earth and the sky, a realm that belongs to you and is safe from anxiety. You claim this realm as yours in which to dream. This is your dreamscape, where you float towards rest and sleep. Your realm is one of peace that connects the heavens with the ground. It is yours alone to govern, to allow only positive energy and love. You roam over the tops of trees, drift across the width of lakes, and coast above others, sleeping in their warm beds.

Your entire body now is floating higher and higher in this realm as you feel such elation inside as you realize you are now gliding through all of space. You are drifting and roaming here, no longer bound by gravity. You are now soaring like a hot air balloon, ascending higher and moving towards infinity of this welcoming expands. As you float you are letting go of everything that you no longer need. You toss away unwanted negativity. You hold on to the comfort that peace grants you.

Your entire body now is floating higher and higher in this realm as you feel such elation inside as you realize you are now gliding through all of space. You are drifting and roaming here, no longer bound by gravity. You are now soaring like a hot air balloon, ascending higher and moving towards infinity of this welcoming expands. As you float you are letting go of everything you no longer need. You toss away unwanted negativity. You hold on to the comfort that peace grants you. As you become just like the pure brilliance of the stars, a beautiful shining light, you feel your spirit break free and finally you are able to float out through the entire universe. You reach out further and further into the purest wisdoms, and the most loving embraces of all of the celestial beings that surround you. They are calling you to rest, to dream, to sleep, to heal. You feel yourself realigning from within.

You feel yourself moving with tranquility and mindfulness, further and further. As you wade through the stars, you feel yourself gently feeling heavier. You understand that you are drifting towards rest.

You drift through the cosmos, feeling gravity's kind tug towards the ground. Gently you float towards the earth like a leaf falls from a tree, eager to meet its rest on the ground below. You feel completely relaxed and slipping away into a restful sleep. Before you escape into your dreams, you return to your bed where you are warm and protected. Your body softly nestles under the blankets and your head snuggles into the pillow. You notice your arms and legs still feel weightless and there is a residual warm vibration throughout, a pulsing that beseeches sleep. You happily oblige.

I am going to count down from five. When I reach one, you are going to fully embrace the peace that has engulfed you and lose yourself in sleep. You will feel yourself slipping into a calm and serene rest.

Five... You think of the night sky and its expansiveness. It melts away every remaining tension until your body and mind are relaxed. It is summoning your sleep.

Four... You feel the warmth of peace move from the top of your head and down your neck. It moves through your shoulders, radiates through your chest and stomach, and finally glazes over your legs.

Three... You feel your body become heavy and you softly sink in a little deeper to your consciousness. You are safe and protected.

Two... You feel yourself drift away, like a leaf on a still pond. You float away, quietly into the night.

One... You are now asleep, resting and at peace.

Breathe in, breathe out. Breathe in, breathe out. When you wake, you will be refreshed and ready to take on the day. You will be ready to conquer the stresses of your life now that you have conquered sleep.

Conclusion

E ven though anxiety can be difficult to manage, people should not feel like they have to struggle with it forever. The first step to recovery is often acknowledging its many symptoms such as sweating, trembling, a racing heart, and nervousness. Making efforts not to let anxious thoughts control your day and decisions can be difficult, but it can help to keep you from having panic attacks. Learning how to ride out the symptoms of anxiety and panic takes a lot of practice and it is important not to get discouraged or start avoiding situations due to anxiety.

Sometimes dealing with anxiety can be too much for someone to handle without professional help. It can be difficult to admit what seems like defeat and call a doctor, but it can be the best way for people with severe symptoms to find relief. There is a wide array of options to choose from when picking a doctor. If a person is too overwhelmed by their choices, they can always go to their primary care doctor who can then refer them to a trusted psychologist or counselor. After establishing a relationship with the therapist, you can then work on establishing trust and working toward a long-term goal with milestones along the way.

It's perfectly astute and correct to assume that this moment within your life may be all that you have. Thus, learn to embrace it and stop feeling bogged down by other people's judgment of you. If you made mistakes in the past, don't make them in this moment and don't waste this moment by letting your thoughts drag you into the past. If you can make things right with people by apologizing, do so. If you can't, learn from the mistake and don't make it again.

Anxiety can go away, but you have to understand that a thought that you have today isn't important in the overall picture of life. If you waste this moment on negative thoughts, you go into the next moment with negativity already there in your life. If you fill this moment with a positive action, you reinforce your value and you move forward into the next moment as a better person than you were a moment ago. Thus, it follows that building up your confidence should be done moment by moment. I made a friend a cup of coffee because I knew that she was lonely. It made her feel better. It made me feel better. Small gestures that take selfish thought out of the picture help to build up positivity that helps to pull you out of the pits of depression. I helped a lady with her shopping because she was older and struggling. When you give, give with no expectations of return because that's the kind of giving that helps you to build up your confidence in yourself. You do things because you know they are positive things to do. You don't do them for thanks or for something given in return. When you incorporate giving into your everyday life, it's a positive reminder to yourself that you have value.

Even after a great loss in your life, you need to feel that value explained above. You may lose your purpose for a while, but if you make this your aim in life, you begin to feel you are building strong roots that will take you through all the pitfalls of life with your head held high, knowing that your personal strength and roots will help you through the bad times that come into your life. Anxiety is a phase. It's a stopping point to reassess who you are and make yourself even stronger and more confident, taking you back up the path to happiness. Whether you are in desperate need of higher self-esteem, or you want to help someone else increase their low self-esteem, you need to be prepared. While we introduced many proven techniques to encourage awareness of the importance of self-esteem, it is up to you, the individual, to take action.

You must be dedicated to giving yourself the tools you need to succeed in this competitive world. You can now experience yourself as a capable individual who can meet life's challenges. You can establish strong, healthy relationships from this moment on. You can develop self-reliance and self-worth.

While there are many life crises that can keep you from maintaining a healthy self-esteem, you certainly do not have to let them. Hold your head high and never forget to believe in yourself.

Account for your own well-being. Start by taking baby steps. Don't waste another minute. Do whatever you can to motivate yourself – for your own sake and for the sake of those around you.

And remember, your happiness (or misery) depends a great deal upon:

- The treatment you accord yourself
- Your worldview
- Your self-talk
- How you start your day
- The goals you set for yourself
- How you interact with others
- How others influence you
- Where your focus is
- Your involvement in social activities

Keep these ideas in mind and work on your self-esteem for the following weeks.

Now that you have the tools to work through these things, it is a journey you must take. It may be difficult at times, but the rewards will be well worth the work. By learning to be optimistic, gaining mental control, and emotional intelligence, you will be able to lead a more positive and happy life.

I hope that you will share this with your friends and family and anyone else you know that may struggle with low self-esteem who wants to make a change. Having people to take this journey with you and support you in your pursuit of gaining self-confidence will be quite beneficial in both of your journeys. Even if you do not share this with others, speaking with them about the struggles you face and opening up to them about your low self-esteem can help you to feel more supported. Having support when working towards something like this is important for those days when it becomes difficult, and you lack motivation.

Having people, you look up to is also beneficial. If there is someone who you look up to in terms of their self-confidence and their self-esteem, they may be able to help you by being a benchmark for where you want to get to with your self-esteem. By seeing them and what they do to maintain a higher level of self-esteem, this could help you to set your own goals for your life. Ensure that this person is someone who you can talk to and who you can share your experience with so that you can get some insight into their everyday life and how it may differ from yours. The more support you have, the better, but even if you don't have this, this journey can be taken on your own, and you will be much stronger for it.

This is just the beginning of your journey to a lasting and fulfilling high self-esteem.

As you begin this journey, you will start to enjoy your life in ways you never have before. You will be doing more of the things you have always wanted to do, and you will find new value in your life.

Don't waste another minute... Get started today!

Lightning Source UK Ltd.
Milton Keynes UK
UKHW052331151220
374938UK00003BA/389

9 781801 256834